THE
ULTIMATE
Tailgater's™
BIG 12
HANDBOOK

YO-DKM-099

STEPHEN LINN

theultimatetailgater.com

[interactive blvd]™

An Interactive Blvd Book
interactiveblvd.com

The Globe Pequot Press

GUILFORD, CONNECTICUT

Copyright © 2007 by 4964 Productions, LLC.

An Interactive Blvd Book. Interactive Blvd is a division of 4964 Productions, LLC.
interactiveblvd.com.

Design by Karen Williams [Intudesign.net]

Photographs: Baylor: Rod Aydelotte, Colorado: Cliff Grassmick, Iowa State: Jon Britton, Kansas: Mike Yoder, Kansas State: Pete Aiken, Missouri: L.G. Patterson, Nebraska: Gwyneth Roberts, Oklahoma: Lisa Hall, Oklahoma State: Jessica Blackburn, Texas: Laura Harris, Texas A&M: Bill Meeks, Texas Tech: Joe Don Buckner.

Special thanks to Barb Rishaw, Steve Ney, Ed Rode, Shanon Davis, Karen Williams, and Scott Adams for all of their help and support with this project.

Library of Congress Cataloging-in-Publication Data is available on file.

ISBN 978-0-7627-4497-8

Manufactured in the United States of America

First Edition/First Printing

TABLE OF CONTENTS

THE BIG 12

The Big 12 is home to some powerhouse football programs, some of the most loyal (and vocal) fans in the country, and some of the biggest tailgate parties in America. And some great barbecue, too (you'll learn more about that in the recipe chapter).

The Big 12's been around for 100 years. Sort of. There were a lot of moving parts during the century, so follow me as I walk through all of this; it can get confusing. And if you're not good with numbers, you may want to grab a pencil.

In January 1907 the University of Kansas, the University of Missouri, the University of Nebraska, and the University of Washington at St. Louis formed the Missouri Valley Intercollegiate Athletic Association (MVIAA). The University of Iowa was a joint member of the MVIAA, but it was also a member of the Western Conference, which became part of the Big Ten. In 1908 Iowa became just a Big Ten school.

Iowa may have left, but that

BIG 12 HEISMAN TROPHY WINNERS	
1952	Billy Vessels, Oklahoma
1957	John Davis Crow, Texas A&M
1969	Steve Owens, Oklahoma
1972	Johnny Rogers, Nebraska
1977	Earl Campbell, Texas
1978	Billy Sims, Oklahoma
1983	Mike Rozier, Nebraska
1988	Barry Sanders, Oklahoma State
1994	Rashaan Salaam, Colorado
1998	Ricky Williams, Texas
2001	Eric Crouch, Nebraska
2003	Jason White, Oklahoma

same year Drake University and Iowa State College (now Iowa State University) joined the conference. Kansas State University came onboard in 1913.

The end of the decade saw Nebraska leave the MVIAA in 1919 (to become an independent), and Grinnell College filled its void. In 1920 Oklahoma joined the conference, and in 1921 Nebraska came home and rejoined. Oklahoma A&M (now Oklahoma State University) became a part of the MVIAA in 1925.

Just as things settled down, they changed again when, in 1928, the conference split up.

The big state schools—Kansas, Kansas State, Missouri, Nebraska, Iowa State, and Oklahoma—stayed in the MVIAA, and the rest formed the Missouri Valley Conference (MVC). Since the two conferences had such similar names, and both claimed to begin in 1907, the MVIAA became known as the Big 6 Conference to fans and the media.

The Big 6 became the Big 7 in 1948 when Colorado joined (from the Skyline Conference). Oklahoma State "rejoined" in 1958—it had gone to the MVC—to create the Big 8. That name became the official conference name in 1964.

While all of this was going on, the Southwest Conference was growing in Texas, Oklahoma, and Arkansas. In fact, Oklahoma and Oklahoma State had been members before moving to the MVIAA. But by the mid-1990s the SWC was struggling, and it dissolved in 1994. Baylor University, the University of Texas, Texas A&M University, and Texas Tech University joined the Big 8, making it the Big 12. The Big 12's first football season as a new conference was 1996.

Big 12 fans have cheered five conference teams to national championships since 1939 (Texas, Texas A&M, Oklahoma, Nebraska, and Colorado), and a dozen Big 12 players have taken home college football's most coveted individual award—the Heisman Trophy.

VENUE AND PRICING GUIDES

For each city in the Big 12, I've included a campus snapshot that includes a tailgating venue guide. That's what all the icons are; use the chart below to learn what you can and can't do outside the stadium. At the time this book was printed all of the information was correct; but things can change, so be sure to check the school's Web site or call ahead if you have any questions.

For restaurants and attractions in the area, I've included a pricing guide to help you manage your budget. A quick note about the suggestions for things like restaurants and hotels: as a rule, I haven't included chains in the list. I figure you can find a Denny's or Hilton on your own. I've included suggestions for places unique to the city that you won't find anywhere else.

 Decorations are allowed, excluding banners and signs that are advertising services or goods.

 Alcohol is permitted for those of legal drinking age.

 Grills or cookers are permitted for noncommercial use only.

 Parking is more than $50 per day for cars or larger vehicles.

 Parking is between $30 and $50 per day for cars or larger vehicles.

 Parking is no more than $30 per day for any vehicle.

 RVs may park overnight before or after the game.

 Number of hours you can tailgate before game. Times exceeding 4 hours are included in "4" icon.

 Number of hours you may remain after the event. Usually this includes tailgating, but read the entry to be sure.

 RVs, limos, and other oversized vehicles are allowed.

 Tents may be erected.

 Tables, chairs, and other tailgating furniture are allowed.

 Venue offers visible security presence in parking and tailgating areas.

 Venue offers at least one paved parking lot.

 Shuttle service is available from parking or tailgating areas to the event and back again.

Pricing Guide for Restaurants and Attractions

Restaurants (based on average entrée price):
$	$1–$19
$$	$20–$39
$$$	$40+

Attractions (based on average general admission price):
$	$1–$9
$$	$10–$19
$$$	$20+

BAYLOR

Baylor University: 13,975 students
Waco, TX: pop. 113,726
Floyd Casey Stadium: seats 50,000
Colors: Green and Gold
Nickname: Bears
Mascot: Judge Joy Reynolds and Judge Sue
Sloan (live), Bruiser (costumed), Judge (inflatable)
Phone: (254) 710-3804, (254) 829-0698, I-35 RV Park & Resort

Visiting RVs can't park on campus. Go to I-35 RV Park & Resort for $21–24 a day; resort rules apply. Cars can park on campus, $10 per game. Visitors can also picnic at Creekside Tailgate area (no vehicles here). Tailgating starts at 8 a.m., stops at beginning of game. University has chairs, tables, grills to rent if needed. No alcohol allowed on campus. Heavy police presence deals swiftly with public drunk-and-disorderly fans.

Shuttle Info: Shuttles run from Bill Daniel Student Center to Touchdown Alley starting 2 hours prior to kickoff. No shuttles available for non-student fans.

Bears Media Partners: 1660-AM KRZI

Baylor University is the oldest higher education institution in Texas and the largest Baptist university in the world.

It was also chartered by another country.

In 1845 President Anson Jones of The Republic of Texas (it was a country then) chartered the school, which opened in the town of Independence. Matthews Hopkins and Judge R. E. B. Baylor were two of the school's founders. The story goes that they wanted to name the school for Hopkins's brother, John, but learned another university had already taken that name. Their backup was Baylor.

By 1885 Independence was declining as other Texas towns began to grow thanks, in part, to their proximity to new railroads. Waco was one of those towns, and Baylor packed up and made the 100-mile move to its new hometown.

But it was 100 miles the other direction, in Dallas, where what many consider Baylor's most prominent program was founded. Ironically, it was in the field John Hopkins is famous for.

In 1900 three physicians founded the University of Dallas Medical Department. There wasn't a University of Dallas (although the Catholic Church founded one in 1953, but it is unrelated to this effort), but they used the name anyway. Three years later Baylor bought the medical school and changed the name to the Baylor College of Medicine. In 1943 Dallas city leaders wanted to grow the facility but would agree to help fund it only if Baylor would sever its ties to the Baptist General Convention of Texas. Baylor refused and moved the College of Medicine to Houston. However, the Baylor University Medical Center still operates in Dallas.

In 1991 Baylor did change its structure to be less influenced by the Baptist General Convention and its national body, the Southern Baptist Convention.

The story of Baylor's football program has less controversy. Baylor played its first game in 1899 against Toby's Business School and rolled to a 20–0 win. Next up was Texas A&M University; it was a bad loss (33–0) but the start of a rivalry that continues today. Overall that first team went 2-1-1.

Throughout the years Baylor's never been a national power. There have been some good years and bowl game appearances, but when you add it all up BU's basically a .500 program.

The teams considered to be among the best the Bears have had were those coached by Grant Teaff, who led the team from 1972–1992. During those years the Bears had their only 10-win season (10-2 in 1980), appeared in 8 bowl games, and Teaff was named Southwest Conference Coach of the Year 6 times. He was named national Coach of the Year once.

Among the players Teaff coached at Baylor was the man many consider the most dominate middle linebacker of his era—Mike Singletary. Singletary was All-SWC, All-American, and still holds school records for most tackles in a season (232) and for career tackles (662). He went on, of course, to star in the NFL with the Chicago Bears.

School Mascot

In 1914 Baylor's president decided it was time for the university to have a mascot. He went about it the usual way: he asked the student body to vote on one. The winner would get bragging rights and a $5 gold piece.

Several nominations rolled in, including Antelopes, Frogs, and Ferrets. It was a close vote, but Bears edged out the victory over Buffaloes. Doyle Thraikill suggested Bears, pocketed the $5 gold piece, and instantly became the answer to a trivia question.

The first bear to roam the sidelines arrived on campus in 1917. His name was Ted, and he belonged to the Infantry Division stationed at Waco's Camp MacArthur during World War I. When the Infantry Division moved on, it left the bear for Baylor, and a live mascot has represented Baylor ever since.

All of the live mascots have "Judge" in their names in honor of Judge R. E. B. Baylor who founded the school. The two you'll see on game day are Judge Joy Reynolds (referred to simply as Joy) and Judge Sue Sloan (called Lady). They're named for the wives of former school presidents. The two are American black bears, and when not supporting the team they stay in their recently renovated habitat that includes a waterfall, three pools, two dens, and plenty of grass. Nice digs. If you like, you can visit them there; call (254) 710-1011 to learn more.

If you want to visit Bruiser or Judge, you'll need to go to the game. Bruiser, the costumed mascot, roams the stadium energizing fans while Judge, Bruiser's inflatable sibling, tends to hang out on the field.

Game-Day Traditions
Baylor Line

The Baylor Line is the university's football spirit squad. Organized in 1970, it's made up entirely of freshmen who wear jerseys with their graduation year on them (at least the year they expect it to be) along with their nickname (look carefully, there are some good ones). Before the game, the Baylor Line lines up at the end of the field and on cue runs to positions on the field to create a tunnel the players run through when *they* take the field. The Baylor Line then runs to its reserved spot on the 50-yard line of the visitors' side of the field to watch the game and cheer the Bears.

The squad's name comes from the other "Baylor Line," the school's alma mater. The group was all-male until 1993 when women were allowed to join. Until then female freshmen were a separate group called the Baylor Sidelines.

Bear Claw and "Sic 'Em Bears"

It was a tradition of the Southwest Conference—Baylor's conference before moving to the Big 12—for schools to have hand signs. Texas's Hook 'Em Horns and Texas A&M's Gig 'Em are perhaps the best known, but Baylor has the Bear Claw.

It was introduced in the 1960s by Baylor's yell leaders and is formed by holding up your hand and slightly curving all five fingers to form the claw. To go with the hand sign, leaders also created the "Sic 'Em Bears" yell, which students shout while waving their "claws."

Baylor Fight Song

Bear down you Bears of old Baylor U
We're all for you, GO BEARS!
We're gonna show dear old Baylor
spirit through and through
We're gonna fight them with all our
might, you Bruins bold
And win all our victories for the Green
and Gold.

B-A-Y-L-O-R, Baylor Bears Fight.

Visiting Baylor

Waco is named for the Wacos (sometimes spelled Huecos) who lived on the land where downtown now stands. The Wichita Native American group was forced to leave by the Cherokees in the 1830s. Waco is also where, in 1885 at Morrison's Old Corner Drug Store, a German pharmacist named Charles Alderton created a concoction you know as Dr. Pepper. In addition to being a college town, it has become a media town during the past few years as journalists from around the world make Waco their temporary home as they cover the "Crawford White House" when President George W. Bush is visiting his ranch (it's about 20 minutes from Waco).

Where to Stay

❶ The Brazos House Bed & Breakfast: This century-old brick home has graceful first and second-story porches and was built with bricks made alongside the Brazos River. Even the tin roof is original. Five individually decorated guest rooms are available at this popular B&B, both in the main house and in separate cottages. Guest rooms each come with a private bath, cable TV,

phone, queen-size bed, and robes. Rooms are $80–$120, depending on the day of the week. (*(254) 754-3565, thebrazoshouse.com*) ❷ Colcord House Bed & Breakfast: This Georgian-style brick home is only 10 minutes from Baylor. There are four guest rooms and one suite available, all with cable TV and private baths. The suite is located in the carriage house and comes equipped with a kitchenette and private patio. A full, hot breakfast is served on weekends, with a continental-style breakfast available on weekdays. An outdoor pool is also available. Rooms run $75–$110. (*(254) 753-6856, colcordhouse.com*) ❸ Cotton Palace Bed & Breakfast: This pretty Arts and Crafts style house has seven rooms, including suites and a carriage house, and is nicely furnished. Guest rooms have air conditioning, private baths with whirlpool tubs, cable TV, VCRs, phones, robes, and upscale toiletries. A full gourmet breakfast is served each morning, and cookies and beverages are available all day long. Business services and high-speed Internet are available, too. Rooms run $109–$139 and require a two-night stay during football weekends. (*(877) 632-2312, thecottonpalace.com*) ❹ Hotel Waco: This independently owned hotel/motel near campus offers 170 guestrooms, all newly remodeled. Guests get the standard amenities—coffee maker, hair dryer, high speed and/or wireless Internet, etc.—and the hotel is pet-friendly (with some restrictions). A

complimentary hot breakfast is included in the room rate, which is $99 except during homecoming weekend; then it will cost you $135. (*(866) 953-0261, hotelwaco.com*) ❺ **I-35 RV Park:** Just north of Waco, this park has 215 sites, all with full utility hookups. Sites are large and level; some are covered for extended stays. There's a restaurant on-site that serves some pretty decent food. If you don't want to hang out by the lake, you can enjoy the new pool and spa area. What you won't find here are cable TV and wireless Internet. Sites are $21–$24. (*(254) 829-0698, I35rvpark.com*)

Where to Eat

TAILGATER SUPPLIES: ❶ **Waco Farmers' Market:** This small market runs until the end of September at the Heart o' Texas Fairgrounds and is open on Tuesday, Thursday, and Saturday. The fairground also has special events, rodeos, and other attractions, so check their schedule. (*(254) 357-2570, hotfair.com*)

SPORTS BARS: ❷ **George's Restaurant:** This Baylor institution goes way, way back, providing students and alums with cold beer and game day hijinks as far back as the 1930s. It's a pretty good spot for non-game days, too. George's signature drink is the Big O, an 18-ounce goblet of beer. More recently, the equally large Big Margarit-O has given the Big O a run for its money. You'll want to try their food, which includes burgers and sandwiches, seafood, and Tex-Mex. On game days, George's sets up a tailgate tent directly across the street from the stadium. (*$, (254) 753-1421, georgesrestaurant.com*) ❸ **The Pump Station Sports Bar & Grill:** Originally built to bring water to Waco, today this mid-19th-century brick structure serves liquids a bit stronger than H_2O. Set along the Brazos River, it uses elements from Waco's historic past to great effect—the former cellar, dungeon (yes, dungeon), and boiler room now accommodate drinking, dancing, TV-watching (there're about 20 monitors), live comedy, bands, and more. (*$, (254) 756-7867*)

RESTAURANTS: ❹ **1424 Restaurant:** This restaurant is fast becoming one of Waco's favorites, thanks to a creative menu and an eclectic atmosphere that's both upscale and laid-back at the same time. It's an intimate, one-chef operation here, so reservations are a wise idea. You should also expect a leisurely pace to your meal. Menu choices range from thick, juicy Texas steaks to a tongue-tingling seafood curry. They also offer a patio dining area. (*$–$$, (254) 752-7385*) ❺ **Buzzard Billy's:** Now a chain boasting several locations, Waco's is the

original. With its concrete floors and vintage advertising memorabilia, the décor is rather industrial-casual. Billy's specializes in Cajun and Creole classics, like crawfish étouffée, fried alligator, voodoo tuna, jambalaya, and po' boys. You can also order pastas, steaks, blackened fish, and a variety of sandwiches and starters. If you've got kids, have them check out the gameroom's pool tables and video games while waiting for dinner. (*$, (254) 753-2778, buzzardbillys.com*)

❻ **Northwood Inn:** This elegant restaurant, sheltered by enormous live oak trees, is considered one of Waco's best places for a special-occasion dinner. The menu includes Continental-style dishes like chateaubriand, Sonoran-stuffed quail, and rack of lamb. Service is part of the experience here with tableside preparations. Be sure to explore their great wine list. Guys, you'll want to wear a jacket (and I don't mean the one with the Bears logo on the back). (*$$–$$$, (254) 755-8666, the-northwood-inn.com*) ❼ **Siete Mares:** Don't let its humble exterior fool you. Inside you'll find an entirely different class of Mexican cuisine, one that doesn't rely on the same old burritos. This is cuisine from Southern Mexico—very seafood-centric and full of interesting seasonings. It's a popular restaurant with locals, and a White House Press Corp favorite when the president's in town. Now, pay attention to the rest of this sentence: refills on chips and salsa are not free, so consider yourself warned; and it's BYOB, so bring your beer or wine with you because you can't buy anything harder than a soft drink. (*$, (254) 714-1297*)

Daytime Fun

❶ **Homestead Heritage:** If the Amish and Shakers ever merged lifestyles, the result might look like Homestead Heritage. This 510-acre settlement a few miles outside Waco is a working farm with traditional low-tech methods, much like the Amish. In the Shaker tradition, residents are skilled craftspeople, creating pottery, handcrafted furniture, wrought iron, quilts, handmade brooms and baskets, and more. It's all on display (and for sale) at the visitor's center. You'll also find their Homestead Farms Deli & Bakery, with daily lunch specials, smoked barbecued brisket, and homemade ice cream. Visitors can take a free self-guided tour. Group tours (at least six people) are available if you call ahead. (*$, (254) 754-9600, homesteadheritage.com*) ❷ **Mayborn Museum Complex:** Part of Baylor University, the museum complex is designed to offer engaging learning opportunities to visitors of all ages. The exhibits and educational programs encourage families to learn together and design their own museum experiences. The complex offers 16 hands-on discovery zones with themes ranging from critters to optics and sound. Natural history exhibits are located both indoors and outdoors and include walk-in dioramas with wooly mammoths (among other animals) and exploration stations. There's also a 13-acre Historic Village giving visitors a look at life in Texas from the late 1800s into the early 20th century. The complex also includes a traveling exhibit hall, a theater, a museum store, and a café. (*$ (254) 710-1110, maybornmuseum.com*) ❸ Spirit

of the Rivers Riverboat: A true stern-wheeler, the Spirit cruises through downtown Waco, Baylor University, and Cameron Park, under the historic Waco Suspension Bridge, past the Texas Ranger Hall of Fame and Museum, pretty much through or past all of Waco's highlights. Most cruises throughout the week are at 7 p.m. But Saturdays and Sundays offer 2 p.m. cruises, while later, 8:30 p.m. cruises are offered on Fridays and Saturdays. There's also a Saturday dinner cruise at 6:30 p.m. for $30 per person. Other cruises are $6 to $10 a piece. (*$–$$, (254) 755-7797*)

Nighttime Fun

❶ Club Fusion: Formerly Club Jaguarr, this revamped club has taken Waco by storm, with a large dance floor, several video screens, three bars, VIP areas, pool tables, video games, and even dance cages. Fusion also has impressive sound and light systems helping create a throbbing party environment. Live bands play Sunday evenings. (*$–$$, (254) 690-0002, clubfusiontexas.com*) ❷ Cricket's Grill & Bar: This downtown draft house is a favorite with everyone from families to college kids. Full of dark woods and a comfortable ambience, it has more than

100 beers on tap—everything from Texas microbrews to international favorites. Pair your brew with some of Cricket's burgers, pizzas, fajitas, or chicken fried steak. You can also enjoy Cricket's pool, darts, video games, and shuffleboard. There's even a cigar bar in the back. (*$, (254) 754-4677, cricketsgrill.com*)

❸ **Scruffy Murphy's:** There's nothing better than a good dive bar. This is one of them. There's nothing too high-falutin' about this laid-back hangout. Murphy's friendly beer prices, handful of pool tables, and spacious patio make folks feel right at home, and karaoke is a favorite pastime on Wednesdays. Occasionally, live music is available. TVs and video games also provide some fun. (*$, (254) 753-0802, scruffymurphys.com*)

Shopping

❶ **Baylor University Bookstore:** Located on campus, this is where you'll find anything and (almost) everything with a bear or BU on it. From shot glasses to car magnets, it's all here. (*(254) 710-2161, bkstr.com/Home/10001-10068-1?demoKey=d*) ❷ **RiverSquare Center:** This area used to be the site of a turn-

of-the-century hardware emporium and several warehouses. Today it's home to some of Waco's top restaurants and unique shopping. Upscale boutiques feature home decor, children's clothing, art, apparel, gifts, antiques, and collectibles. The complex sits in the middle of downtown and isn't far from the Brazos River. (*Located at the corner of Franklin Ave. and 4th St. one block from the Brazos River*) ❸ **Sironia:** On Waco's old-time main street, Austin Avenue, this 12,000-square-foot store is home to 41 unique shops including jewelry, gardening, clothing, antiques, and collectibles. A great browsing venue, it also offers a tea room that's perfect for nibbling something while recharging your shopping batteries. Fans of TLC's *Trading Spaces* will want to drop by designer Christi Proctor's design firm and jewelry store here. (*(254) 754-8009*) ❹ **Treasure City Flea Market:** If you're a bargain hunter, you'll want to check out the deals at Treasure City. If you wander the aisles of this old drive-in theater, you'll get a taste for the local scene. Stand-bys at Treasure City include discount clothing, fresh produce, and assorted cast-offs that could be just the treasure you've been seeking. (*(254) 752-5632*)

COLORADO

University of Colorado: 27,954 students
Boulder, CO: pop. 97,673
Folsom Stadium: seats 53,750
Colors: Silver, Gold, and Black
Nickname: Buffaloes
Mascot: Ralphie (live), Chip (costumed)
Phone: (303) 492-7384

Parking and tailgating lots open 10:30 a.m. game day. RVs and oversized vehicles park in Lot 470; pay $20 per spaces needed (RVs need 3, cars need 1, limos 2). There is no overnight parking. Tailgating can continue throughout game. Open containers only allowed inside tailgating areas.

Shuttle Info: All parking and tailgating within easy walking distance. No shuttles needed.

Buffaloes Media Partner: 850-AM KOA

In 1861 the Colorado legislature decided to build Colorado University, and the fight was on. The combatants were about a dozen cities that wanted the school built within its borders. They all worked the floor, but when lawmakers tallied their votes Boulder had won.

Like many western states at the time, there were not many students who were prepared to go to college. So when the university opened in 1877, they moved the entire student body and faculty of Boulder High School into the university's preparatory school. The 1877 prep school graduates became the 1878 Colorado freshman class.

It was not a big school then. In fact, the entire university, from the classrooms to the living quarters of the university's president, was housed in Old Main. The school grew, of course, and experienced a surge of enrollment after World War I when soldiers returned home. Not long afterward Colorado began a challenging period.

It began in the 1920s when the Ku Klux Klan gained control of the state legislature. The Klan and its members in the legislature demanded Colorado dismiss all Catholic and Jewish faculty members from the campus. George Norlin was the university's president at the time, and he refused the request. To force the issue the legislature cut the university's budget to zero. Norlin still refused and guided the school through its financial and political struggles until 1926 when the Klan lost control of the legislature and governorship.

But it wasn't long before Norlin had to face a different economic crisis: the Great Depression. Colorado survived, and many feel Norlin's stewardship helped create the culture that allowed Colorado to grow into one of the great public universities in the country. In 2000 the school was added to the list of "Public Ivy" schools that provide an Ivy League education at a public school price.

Colorado's football team has provided fans excitement for more than 100 years. Its first team took the field in 1890, although its style of play resembled rugby more than football. But by 1894 the team was winning conference championships (it was in the Colorado Football Association then). Colorado has played in five conferences and has won championships in all of them.

In 1990 it won the national championship, although it shared the title with Georgia Tech, which had gone undefeated that year. Colorado lost one game in

1990. It almost lost two but was the beneficiary of an officiating error now infamously known as "The Fifth Down."

The 12th-ranked Buffaloes were at Missouri to take on the unranked Tigers. The lead had gone back and forth all day. With less than a minute left in the game, Colorado was behind but within yards of the go-ahead score. As the Buffalos tried to get into the end zone, the officials lost track of how many plays Colorado had run, and in the confusion the Buffs scored on what was actually their fifth down to beat Mizzou 33–31. The series of downs is on many lists as one of the most memorable moments in college football history.

The 1994 season was also a historic one for the program and running back Rashann Salaam. Salaam rushed for 2,055 yards that season, making him the fourth college back in history to break the 2,000-yard mark. It also impressed those who voted for the Heisman Trophy, which Salaam won that year.

School Mascot

Until 1934 if you referenced the Colorado football team, it was probably by calling them the Silver and Gold, the Big Horns, the Frontiersmen, or any number of other informal nicknames.

But the lure of a $5 prize changed all of that when the student newspaper held a contest to select an official mascot for the team. Two entrants suggested

Buffaloes, which the newspaper's staff selected as the winner. History is unclear if they each won the prize or had to settle for $2.50 each.

The first live mascot made its game-day appearance for the last game of the 1934 season. It was a rental. It cost $25 to hire the animal and a cowboy for the day. It took the cowboy and four students to keep the animal under control.

Live mascots were used off and on until 1966 when a six-month-old calf name Ralph was donated to the school. Not long after that they realized he was a she and Ralph became Ralphie. Ralphie's been around ever since.

Ralphie IX is the half-ton mascot that leads the team onto the field now, and she's a lucky buffalo (actually, it's a bison, but that discussion is for a different book). She was raised on Ted Turner's farm and donated to the school. If she hadn't been she may have been headed for Ted's Montana Grill—the

media mogul's restaurant that features bison dishes.

Chip is the other Buffaloes mascot, but you won't confuse his running around in his costume with Ralphie's pregame stampede. Although Chip is better at leading cheers.

Game-Day Traditions
Old Main Bell

The original bell was cast in 1877 and hung in the belfry of Old Main the next year. For nearly a half-century its purpose was to signal class changes and celebrate Colorado victories. Then it cracked while ringing to celebrate the Buffs gridiron victory over the Colorado School of Mines. So they quit ringing it for class changes. You have to have priorities.

Since then the bell's been replaced twice and used for several student pranks (one of which had the bell missing for two years) but still rings after CU wins. To hear it just head over to the CU Heritage Center after the game. It rings once for every Buffaloes score.

Colorado Fight Song

"Fight CU"

Fight CU down the field,
CU must win
Fight, fight for victory
CU knows no defeat
We'll roll up a mighty score
Never give in
Shoulder to shoulder
We will fight, fight
Fight, fight, fight!

Visiting Colorado

Boulder is the type of college town you see in the movies. In addition to students there's a unique mix of people here, from enviro-hippies to lawyers, Buddhists to artists. The outdoors plays a big role in life here year-round. Of course, winter sports are what the area is known for, and the view from Flagstaff Mountain is a memorable one.

Where to Stay

❶ **The Alps:** In the 1880s this was a stagecoach stop. Now it's a place for you to sleep. And eat. Each of the 12 rooms at this B&B is named for a different

Colorado mining town and has a Jacuzzi or antique claw-footed tub and private balcony or patio. All rooms have working fireplaces, queen beds, and individual thermostats. Rooms run $99–$274, depending on the season. (*(800) 414-2577, alpsinn.com*) ❷ **Boulder Outlook Hotel & Suites:** This place is very "Boulder" with chlorine-free indoor pools, climbing rocks, an enclosed pet park, and a dog-walking service. Plus it's across the street from campus. The Adventure Concierge Service will help you schedule outdoor adventure activities based on your proficiency level. Rooms run $75. (*(800) 542-0304, boulderoutlook.com*) ❸ **The Briar Rose:** Part-owned by a Zen Buddhist monk, the 10 guest rooms here have several business amenities such as modem hookups, large worktables, and bright lighting. Two rooms have fireplaces, and four of the rooms in the carriage house have either a patio or balcony. Rates are $129–$159. (*(888) 786-8440, briarrosebb.com*) ❹ **Dakota Ridge RV Park:** It's located in Golden, about a 20-minute drive south of Boulder, but it offers all the usual amenities, including wireless Internet, as well as landscaped pads. Some of those amenities, such as electric hookups, are charged a la carte, but they cost just a couple of bucks each. If you have a big tailgate crew, this could be your place, as they offer discounts to RV groups of 10 or more.

Sites run $36 before the a la carte add-ons. (*(800) 398-1625, dakotaridgerv.com*)

❺ **Hotel Boulderado:** This historic hotel is one block away from the popular Pearl Street Pedestrian Mall. Its ornate decorations include original pieces from when it opened in 1909. It's an older hotel, so be prepared for smaller rooms, and there's no pool or workout room. On the other hand, the hotel's restaurant, Q, is ranked as one of Boulder's best. Rooms run $195–$365. (*(800) 433-4344, boulderado.com*)

Where to Eat

TAILGATER SUPPLIES: ❶ **Boulder County Farmers' Market:** You'll find everything from fruits and vegetables to wine and cheese here. You should; it's the state's largest farmers' market. Lots of organic foods here, too. The market is open from April to November, but call for times. (*(303) 910-2236, boulderfarmers.org*)

SPORTS BARS: ❷ **Barrel House:** A perennial "Best Sports Bar in Boulder" winner in local newspaper contests. Nearly 40 TVs on the walls and 25 beers on tap (including a lot of Colorado microbrews) will win you contests. It's a long-time meeting place before Buffaloes games, so expect a crowd. (*$, (303) 444-9464*) ❸ **Lazy Dog Sports Bar and Grill:** The televisions scattered all over the place helped it win a "Best of Boulder" title for sports bars. The Portabella mushrooms, baby back ribs, and salmon steaks on the menu helped it win a "Best of Boulder" title for "Best Sports Bar for Food." The Lazy Dog sports two 10-foot TV screens and plenty of Colorado fans, too. (*$$, (303) 440-3355, thelazydog.com*)

RESTAURANTS: ❹ **Casa Alvarez:** It's Mexican food, but not the cheese-covered burritos and combo plates many places serve. Instead you'll find creative seafood, lamb, and pork dishes and a quartet of award-wining chile sauces. (*$, (303) 546-0630, casaalvarezboulder.com*) ❺ **Frasca Food and Wine:** Some of the chefs here come from the French Laundry in California (and if you think that's a fancy Laundromat you need to pick up a copy of *Gourmet*), and their dishes have much of Boulder talking. The menu focuses on Northern Italian cuisine including handmade gnocchi, meats, and fish. The wine cellar houses more than 200 varieties. (*$$$, (303) 442-6966, frascafoodandwine.com*) ❻ **Glacier Homemade Ice Cream:** Chef Mark makes about 80 flavors of ice cream and gelato every day. Pastries, too. These award-winning scoops are a

Boulder favorite for ice cream no matter what the temperature is outside. (*$*, *(303) 440-6542, glacierhomemadeicecream.com*) ❼ **The Kitchen:** Upscale versions of French and Italian peasant fare are on the menu at this simply decorated but lively café. For breakfast you'll find dishes such as organic poached eggs with a side of sautéed wild mushrooms and homemade granola. (*$$, (303) 544-5973, thekitchencafe.com*) ❽ **L'Atelier:** It's small (just 50 seats), but it is what owner-chef Radek Cerny calls his "studio/workshop." He is known for preparing dishes with lots of edible eye appeal that also taste good, including selections such as Pork with Foie Gras and Apple Hennessey and Big Eye Tuna Asiatique. (*$$, (303) 442-7233, latelierboulder.com*)

Daytime Fun

❶ **Boulder Museum of Contemporary Art:** Founded in 1972 by local artists to showcase works by local artists, the BMoCA has grown into an acclaimed museum showcasing local, national, and international art. What you'll see runs from design to graffiti, painting to mixed media. There's also a theater that presents various styles of performances. (*$, (303) 443-2122, bmoca.org*)

❷ **Boulder Reservoir:** This one-acre reservoir is a popular place for swimming (there's a beach), boating, and picnicking (they have some grills). You can rent several types of watercraft including canoes, kayaks, paddle boats, and sailboards. (*$, (303) 441-3456, bouldercolorado. gov/index.php?option=com_content &task=view&id=1267&Itemid=459*)

❸ **Celestial Seasonings Tour:** Celestial Seasonings started when Mo Siegel began gathering herbs in the Colorado mountains and has grown into the largest manufacturer and marketer of specialty teas in North America. Their tour shows you how the famous tea company turns leaves on a bush into the drink in your cup. The tour includes the herb garden and a stop in the hair-raising mint room. (*Free, (800) 434-4246, celestialseasonings.com*) ❹ **Chautauqua Park:** Being in Boulder is about being outdoors, and a walk around this foothills park is a popular activity. The hiking trails meander around the park and up to the top of Flagstaff Mountain (a great view). The park is also popular for special events, bird watching, picnics, and just plain relaxing. (*Free, (303) 413-7200, chautauqua.com*)

Nighttime Fun

❶ **Fox Theater:** A local favorite for music from alt-rock to blues, folk to jazz, and more. A lot of local and regional acts take the stage, but touring national acts will also call the Fox home for a night or two. (*$–$$, (303) 443-3399, foxtheatre.com*) ❷ **Pearl St. Pub & Cellar:** You get three for the price of one here. Upstairs is a pub, in the back is the room they use for music, and down in the basement is the pool and foosball room. Some call it a dive, but they also call it fun. (*$, (303) 939-9900*) ❸ **The Sink:** For more than 80 years students (and locals) have piled into the Sink for burgers and beer. On the walls is the off-the-wall artwork of beatnik artists Mike Dormier and Llloyd Kavich, who began drawing the lively, colorful characters sometime in the 1950s. The place is a local legend and across the street from CU. (*$, (303) 444-7465, thesink.com*) ❹ **Soma:** Here it's all about the dancing. DJs spin hip, electronica, cutting-edge dance music while the crowd crowds the floor to show their moves. The dance floor, like the bar, can get crowded on weekends. (*$, (303) 938-8600 or (303) 402-1690 after 7:00 p.m.*)

Shopping

❶ **CU Book Store:** Sure you can get the usual CU swag here, but you can also get Buffs apparel with Cookie Monster or Oscar the Grouch on it. There're collars for your dog and tire covers for your spare. And aprons and sleeping

bags for your tailgate party. The bookstore is in the University Memorial Center on campus. (*(800) 255-9168, cubookstore.com*) ❷ **Pearl Street Pedestrian Mall:** These four, tree-lined blocks along Pearl Street, between 11th and 15th Streets, feature flowers, wooden benches, and sculptures. They also feature shops, galleries, cafés, bookstores, and more. Street musicians, palm readers, jugglers, magicians, and others hang out in front of the county courthouse to entertain you and earn your tips.

IOWA STATE

Iowa State University: 25,741 students
Ames, IA: pop. 50,731
Jack Trice Stadium: seats 45,814
Colors: Cardinal and Gold
Nickname: Cyclones
Mascot: Cy
Phone: (515) 294-3388

RVs can arrive Friday before game, 5 p.m. in Lots G2 and G3 for $30, or Lot 93 for $20. Cars pay $8 to $10 depending on location. Tailgating starts 6 hours prior to game and goes until noon Sunday, when everyone leaves. No glass bottles allowed; leave kegs, funnels, and beer balls at home. Canopies must be no larger than 10 x 10 feet.

Shuttle Info: Free shuttles provided throughout parking areas to stadium complex. Shuttles start 3 hours prior to kickoff, end 1 hour after game's conclusion.

Cyclones Media Partners: 1430-AM KASI, 105.1-FM KCCQ

In 1858 the state of Iowa paid $5,379 for 648 acres of farmland in Story County, Iowa. That was to be the home of the State Agricultural College and Model Farm. The first building was finished in 1861, about the same time the state decided to participate in the Morrill Act, which provided federal funds for states willing to create universities teaching agricultural and mechanical curriculums.

So the state regrouped, renamed the school Iowa State College of Agricultural and Mechanic Arts, and expanded its focus. The first students started class in 1869. (In 1959 the school was renamed Iowa State University of Science and Technology, which is still its formal name.)

The school grew during its early years, adding buildings and students. But 1894 and 1895 brought trouble. During those years a string of powerful tornadoes hit Iowa, causing a great deal of damage. If it wasn't wind, it was water, or lack of it, that caused problems. The water shortage of 1895 was so bad it forced ISU to cancel classes and build the Marston Water Tower, which was the first elevated steel water tank west of the Mississippi.

It was at this same time that Iowa State's first black student, and later the first black faculty member, came to campus, George Carver. There was another George Carver in his classes, however, so he began to use the name George Washington Carver. He left Iowa State in 1896 for the Tuskegee Institute where he led the Agriculture Department for 47 years until his death in 1943. At Tuskegee he became famous, of course, for his work teaching former slaves farming techniques to become self-sufficient and promoting alternative crops for food and profit like peanuts and sweet potatoes.

Meanwhile, at ISU, the university expanded its curriculum and research, which led the school to develop many patents and inventions including the first binary computer, the round hay baler, and Maytag blue cheese.

Iowa State didn't invent football, but one of its coaches did help reinvent the game. But first, some history.

Football was first played on campus in the late 1870s, but no one much cared. Many considered the game a waste of time. But, apparently, a lot of students liked to waste time because the sport became more popular as an intramural contest, so a field was created, and in 1892 the school's first recorded game was played. (If you're keeping score, it was a 6–6 tie against State Center.)

In 1895 Glenn S. Warner came to campus. He was just beginning his coaching career and came to Iowa State to coach in the late summer before heading off to coach at schools in the East and Southeast. It was at those schools where the man better known as "Pop" Warner amassed 319 wins in his 44-year career (337 wins if you count the 18 he had at ISU, which the record books don't count). This coaching of two teams during the same season—ISU and Georgia in 1895 and 1896, ISU and Cornell in 1897 and 1898, and ISU and Carlisle in 1899—was as innovative as the formations and plays he created such as the screen play, the spiral punt, and the single- and double-wing formations. He also came up with the ideas of numbering players' jerseys and using shoulder and thigh pads.

They may have been primarily preseason drills, but they paid off for the Cyclones, who by 1913 had a combined record of 52-12-4.

Perhaps the most celebrated Cyclone team was the 1959 "Dirty Thirty." That year injuries reduced the ISU squad to just 30 players as the season opened. Nonetheless they opened with a 41–0 win over Drake in a rainy, muddy game. Afterward the trainer announced, "Here comes the Dirty Thirty." The Dirty Thirty went on to post a 7-3 record when most thought ISU would be lucky to get to .500.

School Mascot

In 1895 the Iowa State Cardinals (as they were unofficially called) headed to Northwestern to play the heavily favored Wildcats. At halftime the score was as many expected: 30–0. What no one expected was that Iowa State had scored the 30 points. ISU won the game 36–0, and the next morning's paper reported the outcome under

the headline: "Struck by a Cyclone—Iowa Cyclone Devastates Evanston Town."

The choice of words was not random. Throughout the summer and fall of that year Iowa was hit by an unusually high number of what were then called cyclones that devastated many parts of the state. So the reference was as meaningful as the game was to Iowa State, and the nickname stuck. (If they had known more about weather phenomena at the time, the Iowa State Tornadoes would take the field today.)

But it's not easy to stuff a cyclone character and have it run around the field. That's why a cardinal has that honor.

For nearly 50 years ISU had a nickname but no mascot. A group of students, led by the pep council president, convinced the school to let them come up with a mascot to help build school spirit. They went with a bird based on the school colors of cardinal and gold. The cardinal-like mascot debuted at the 1954 homecoming pep rally.

A contest was held to come up with a moniker for the bird. Seventeen people submitted the winning entry: Cy (short for Cyclones). But only one got the first prize, a cardinal and gold stadium blanket. That reward went to Mrs. Ed Ohlsen; she got her entry in before the other winners.

ISU Fight Song

Oh, we will fight, fight, fight for Iowa State
And may her colors ever fly.
Oh, we will fight with might for Iowa State
With the will to do or die!
Rah, Rah, Rah
Loyal sons forever true
And we will fight that battle through.
And when we hit the line we'll hit it hard, every yard for I-S-U!

Game-Day Traditions
The Victory Bell

Beginning in 1890 students at Iowa State knew it was time to change classes when the big bell rang. But in the years since, the bell has come to symbolize something perhaps more important for Cyclone students and fans: football victories.

In the early 20th century, the bell was moved to Clyde Williams Field, where the Cyclones used to play, and was rung after every football victory. When Jack Trice Stadium was built, the bell was moved again and is still rung after every home win to the cheers of the faithful.

Presidential Cheer

If you want to get the crowd fired up . . . start at the top. It's a new tradition, but 9 minutes before kickoff the president of the ISU Alumni Association leads the crowd in cheers to get them ready for the game. If you want to participate you need to be prepared; it can get complicated since different parts of the stands shout different parts of the cheer. That's why I'm here. Practice these in front of the mirror a few times, and you should be okay:

I-S-U . . . I-S-U . . . I-S-U

(Performed by the entire stadium in unison)

Cyclone-Power . . . Cyclone-Power

(Performed alternately by the east and west sides of the stadium)

CY-CL-ON-ES . . . Cyclones . . . Cyclones . . . Go State

(Performed with the east stands yelling C-Y, the south stands and hillsides yelling C-L, the west stands spelling O-N, and the north stands and hillsides yelling E-S, followed by the entire crowd saying in unison Cyclones . . . Cyclones . . . Go State)

I-S-U . . . Whatcha gonna do? (I-S-U)
I-S-U . . . Whatcha gonna do? (I-S-U)
(Performed by the entire stadium in unison. Cheers done in concert with the band while leaning forward, leaning to the right, leaning back, leaning left, and yelling the letters I-S-U each time you lean backward)

Cardinal-Gold . . . Cardinal-Gold
(Performed alternately by the east and west sides of the stadium)

Let's Go State . . . Let's Go State
(Performed by the entire stadium in unison)

Visiting Iowa State

While it's primarily a college town, there are several manufacturing facilities in Ames including ones for 3M, Pella windows, and Ball, the canning company famous for those old Mason jars (which they don't make anymore). The town was founded

as a stop along the Cedar Rapids and Missouri Railroad and is named for former Massachusetts congressman Oakes Ames who had a leading role in developing the transcontinental railroad.

Where to Stay

❶ **Campus Bed & Breakfast:** Just a stone's throw from ISU's stadium, this B&B has three guest rooms. The feeling and style here is pure Prairie—simple yet cozy, comfy, and warm. All three guest rooms have private baths, although one room's bath is a few feet down the hall. The whole house offers wireless Internet service. Room rates range from $85 for a single to $125 for double occupancy. (*(515) 451-6007, campusbandb.com*) ❷ **Gateway Hotel & Conference Center:** An unexpected gem, rooms are furnished in clean-lined Prairie-style décor, and are more stylish than you'd expect. Rooms have beds with pillow-top mattresses and down comforters, and high-speed Internet. There are other neat touches, like putting a little goldfish in your room if you request it, or use of the hotel's bikes, kites, and even sleds for some rec time. During football weekends, standard rooms are $139, with suites running from $159 to $179. The hotel books up far in advance; it's a good idea to call in early spring for the fall season. (*(800) FOR-AMES, gatewayames.com*)

❸ **Iowa State University Memorial Union:** Located

on the ISU campus, this stately building offers cozy, European-style rooms and suites on its fourth, fifth, and sixth floors. Guest rooms are on the large side, with both wireless and wired Internet available. Guests get free parking, and guest room staff members are available around the clock. During football weekends, rooms are $85 per night, while suites are $95. It's a good deal, but be sure to reserve your room at least two months ahead of time. (*(515) 296-6848, mu.iastate.edu/reservations.php*) ❹ **MontBello Bed & Breakfast Inn:** This B&B offers four guest rooms and a blast of Mexico, just 2 miles south of ISU's campus. The building's interior is decorated with Mexican artwork hung on brightly painted walls; stairs are trimmed in colorful tile work. Guest rooms are large and bright, with private baths and wrought-iron beds. Guests can choose between American- or Mexican-style breakfasts. Rooms run $105 to $115. During football weekends and other big events, advance payment may be required. (*(515) 296-2181, montebellobandbinn.com*) ❺ **Twin Acres Campground:** This campground is roughly 10 miles east of Ames and offers 220 sites with electric hookups; about half of those have water, and one-third offer sewer hookups. Seasonal RV campers fill half the sites, though. Lakeside sites cost $13; the others cost $12. Rural water is $2, sewer $2.50, electric $2 or $4 for 50-amp service, so a site with the works would run $21.50. The only drawback is Twin Acres closes for the winter at the end of October. (*(641) 377-2243*)

Where to Eat

TAILGATER SUPPLIES: ❶ **Wheatsfield Cooperative:** This member-owned organic and natural food store features local produce, gourmet meat and poultry, and bulk products including tea, herbs, spices, liquids, nut butters, and dry goods. The store also carries a large selection of beer and wine, books, supplements, and health and beauty products. Wheatsfield is open to the public (you don't need a membership to shop here), and there's no surcharge for nonmembers. (*(515) 233-0040, wheatsfield.com*)

SPORTS BARS: ❷ Indigo Joe's Sports Pub & Restaurant: This place serves both hardcore sports fans and families. For the sports fans, several HD and plasma TVs play the big games. There are even TVs in the bathrooms, so you won't miss any of the action. Patrons can also get a wireless speaker tuned to a specific TV to listen when the restaurant's crowded. If you're not into the game, you can play trivia with people across the country on the National Trivia Network at your table. The menu has a wide selection of sand-

wiches, entrées that range from ribs to swordfish, and plenty of drink specials. (*$, (515) 232-5637, indigojoes.com*) ❸ **Wallaby's:** This place is a sports fan's dream, with professional and collegiate memorabilia everywhere, including an autographed jersey from Michael Jordan. The bar sits in the center of the room, with 15 big screen televisions ringing the wall above it. No matter where you are, you'll be able to see the game. The menu lists a total of 65 items, all cooked from scratch in the kitchen. Start out with the fried Mozzarella cheese wedges, then order the DeBurgo burger—a half-pound of ground Iowa beef basted in butter. (*$, (515) 292-1167*)

RESTAURANTS: ❹ **Aunt Maude's:** Stained-glass windows, soft lighting, and rich oil paintings create an inviting place to dine. While the menu includes Iowa standbys such as prime rib and sirloin, Maude's also serves up rack of lamb, smoked pork tenderloin, breast of duck, and locally raised free-range chicken. Side dishes are especially creative, and locals say it's worth saving some room to sample their desserts. (*$$, (515) 233-4136*) ❺ **The Café:** This combination bakery and café brings a little bit of Provence to the Midwest. Walls painted in deep, glowing tones of amber and honey give the place a

warm, earthy glow. Much of the menu uses ingredients gathered from local growers. Try the Plowman's Platter appetizer—it's a sampler with a little bit of everything. For an entrée enjoy the Chipotle Rubbed Tri-tip, or the free-range rotisserie chicken. As for dessert, hey, it's a bakery—go nuts. (*$, (515) 292-0100*) ❻ **The Grove Café:** Start your day off with some of the best pancakes you've ever eaten. Located in the old business district, Grove Café is your classic diner with bare-table booths and a low-slung counter in front of the grill. A pancake here is no ordinary flapjack; it's as wide as your plate and nearly an inch thick at the center. The Grove also offers omelets and French toast, as well as hamburgers, hot beef, and meat loaf at lunch—if you're still hungry after breakfast. (*$, (515) 232-9784, grovecafeamesiowa.tripod.com*)

Daytime Fun

❶ **Boone and Scenic Valley Railroad:** This operating railroad museum provides several options for great fun, assuming you love trains. Even if you're not a train buff, it's hard not to like their scenic excursion rides across the Des Moines River Valley, dinner trains, charters, dessert trains, and picnic trains. (The dessert train is very popular—make sure you call ahead for reservations.)

Tickets run from as little as $5 for kids in coach, to $50 for adults on the dinner train. (*$–$$$, (800) 626-0319, scenic-valleyrr.com*) ❷ **Golf:** If you brought your clubs, you'll find more courses in Ames than you may have expected. Among them is **Homewood Golf Course**, a well-groomed 9 hole, par 34 municipal golf course, and ISU's **Veenker Memorial Golf Course**, which was originally a Perry Maxwell design when built in 1938. And if those two don't do it for you, there are three more nearby. (*$–$$, (515) 239-5363 Homewood, (515) 294-6727 Veenker, veenkergolf.com*) ❸ **Iowa State University Museums:** ISU's two museums, the Brunnier Art Museum and the Farm House Museum, combined with the Art on Campus Program, offer a broad variety of art and history. The Art Museum is stuffed with an impressive collection of glass, ceramics, enamels, ivory, and wood objects, along with works from significant Iowa painters, an Asian collection, and 20th-century works of art. The Farm House Museum, a three-story, grey stucco house built in 1860, was the first building on the ISU campus. Inside you'll find 19th- and early 20th-century decorative arts, furnishings, and materials on Iowa State and Iowa. You'll be greeted with free hot cider, lemonade, and comfy wicker chairs on the front porch. (*Free,*

(515) 294-3342 Brunnier Museum, (515) 294-7426 Farm House, museums.iastate.edu) ❹ Prairie Moon Winery & Vineyards: This 18-acre organic vineyard specializes in French varietal grapes, has an elegant new tasting room, and offers interesting tours of their operation. During warmer months bands play on Sunday afternoons, creating a perfect setting for a picnic. ($, (515) 232-2747, prairiemoonwinery.com)

Nighttime Fun

❶ Brewers: This is one of Ames's more upscale bars. Its interior is clean, smoke-free, and stocked with comfortable couches and stools for perching. The emphasis here is on relaxing and conversing; the music is turned down low enough to allow for easy chatting. Brewers also offers a wide selection of wines and martinis, not just the usual brews. ($, (515) 292-0033) ❷ Café Beaudelaire: Famous locally for its excellent Long Island teas, Beaudelaire is a restaurant by day and a bar by night. The menu features Brazilian items, along with regular bar food. If you need to escape the college scene, Beaudelaire offers an atmosphere where internationals and older folks can feel more comfortable. With a DJ playing salsa, merengue, or swing on the weekends, you'll find some of the best dancing in Ames here. ($, (515) 292-7429, cafebeau.com) ❸ Club Element: This hot-spot is a multilevel dance club with a bar on each floor. With the largest laser light show in central Iowa, live DJs, a dance floor, and a 1,200-square-foot outdoor patio overlooking Campustown, you can understand why this is where ISU's party animals go to howl. If you want to join them, come dressed semi-casual and bring your coolitude with you. (*$–$$, feeltheelement.com*) ❹ **The London Underground:** Formerly known as 212 Main, this local favorite has reopened as an English pub. Everything's newly redecorated and snazzy, with great imported beers on tap to keep you happy. While the Underground is fairly quiet and laid back Sunday through Wednesday, Thursday through Saturday it's one busy, happening place. It may have something to do with a happy hour that lasts until 8 p.m. those days. (*$, (515) 233-2040*)

Shopping

❶ **Antique Ames:** If you like nosing around, this downtown antique mall is right up your vintage-loving alley. It's housed in an 11,000-square-foot, restored, turn-of-the-century department store. Their emphasis is on vintage and antique items for home furnishing and décor, so you won't find much in the way of clothing or accessories. But then, how many nylon '70s leisure suits do you really need? (*(515) 233-2519, antiqueames.com/index.cfm*) ❷ **Campus Bookstore:** This is one of two places in town to get anything and everything Cyclone. If you can put an ISU logo on it, you'll probably find it here. They've

got everything from sweatshirts to wall clocks to temporary face tattoos. (*(888) 292-1696, stores.cbsames.net/StoreFront.bok*) ❸ **ISU Bookstore:** This is the other place in town to get your ISU swag. The bookstore has an extensive selection of Cyclone stuff, which you'd expect. But it also has a couple of things you might not—like the eight-piece Iowa State grill set in a snazzy aluminum case, plus lots of other tailgating supplies. (*(800) 478-0048, isubookstore.com/Home.aspx*) ❹ **Octagon Center for the Arts Shop:** This art center features art and craft items by more than 175 regional artists. All are unique, handcrafted items by serious artisans, including pottery, jewelry, fiber, glass, wood, paintings, photography, and just about anything else you can think of. (*(515) 232-5331, octagonarts.org*)

KANSAS

University of Kansas: 29,613 students
Lawrence, KS: pop. 80,098
Memorial Stadium: seats 50,250
Colors: Crimson and Blue
Nickname: Jayhawks
Mascot: Big Jay
Phone: (785) 864-7275

Visitors park for free at Lot 72 or Lot 90, starting Friday at 5 p.m. Tailgating may start upon arrival and ends 2 hours after game time. RVs may stay until Sunday afternoon. Other lots carry a charge of $10. Kegs, beer balls, etc., are forbidden.

Shuttle Info: Catch a ride at Irving Hill Road, just north of Burge Union or the parking lot south of Robinson Center. One way is $2, round trip $3 per person. Shuttle starts 2 hours before kickoff.

Jayhawks Media Partners: 1320-AM KLWN, 105.9-FM KLZR

There's a saying that goes, "If I didn't have bad luck, I wouldn't have any luck at all." That was pretty true for the University of Kansas when it opened its doors in 1866.

For one thing, it was in a territory that was rife with everything from deadly violence and territorial wars to poverty and disease. Then there was the Civil War. Let's just say formal education wasn't high on the priority list for most Kansans. That meant there were not a lot of students ready for college, so in effect KU's early years were as a preparatory school, as was the case for state universities in several western states.

And it was a poor university, too. When the legislature created the University of Kansas, they didn't bother with funding it. In fact the charter absolved the state from any fiscal responsibility for the school. Money was

so tight that the university ran out of it just weeks before it opened. Support from local leaders, including philanthropist Amos Adams Lawrence (for whom the city of Lawrence is named), provided the land and funds the school needed to survive.

It survived and grew, adding facilities and programs that attracted more students and improved the school's reputation. Over the years it's developed into a large liberal arts college.

It's also the place where the man who invented basketball coached. In fact, Dr. James Naismith started the Kansas basketball program. Ironically, the guy who created the game is the only KU basketball coach in history with a losing record.

KU's football team doesn't own a losing record, but overall it's been pretty average with a combined record just above .500.

The first Jayhawkers team, as it was called then, hit the field in 1890. The early years were good ones with KU teams playing well, including a perfect season in 1899.

But the sport almost didn't last past 1910. That was the year members of the Board of Regents proposed abolishing football because, as one board member put it, the sport had come to "stand for brutality, for trickery; for paid players, for profanity, for betting before games and for drinking after them."

This feeling had been brewing for some time. In 1890 an opposing player in a game against Doane College died making a tackle. It wasn't the sport's only fatality nationally, and in an era where players didn't wear much in the way of padding, injuries and death were fairly common.

Also common were stories of teams using ringers and professional players to try and win. It hit home in Lawrence in 1901 when Coach John Outland (who later would have the Outland Trophy named for him) was caught using an ineligible player under an assumed name.

So by 1910 some members of the Board of Regents had had enough. As their proposal to ban football was being debated, the outcome seemed so certain that students were preparing for rugby to take football's place on campus. But the measure failed, some new rules were put in place, and football stayed.

It's a good thing, too, or Jayhawk fans would never have seen Gale Sayers.

"The Kansas Comet" played in Lawrence from 1962 to 1964 and tore up the record books. He led the Jayhawks in almost every offensive category. Sayers went on to play in the NFL for the Chicago Bears and was the youngest player ever inducted into the Pro Football Hall of Fame. He was also the first Jayhawk to make it to the Hall of Fame.

School Mascot

Kansas may be the Jayhawks, but no one is absolutely certain where the word came from. The first use was either 1849 or 1858, depending on which story you believe. And they are very different stories.

The 1849 one recalls a group of pioneers who combined the names of two common birds—the blue jay and the hawk—to create a moniker for themselves as they crossed present-day Nebraska, "The Jayhawkers of '49."

If you believe the other story, you didn't want to be called a Jayhawk. That legend has it that the term was associated with robbery and other forms of general bad behavior and lawlessness.

The story becomes clearer during the Civil War when a colonel raising a regiment of cavalry called his men the Independent Mounted Kansas Jayhawkers (the official name, however, was the First Kansas Cavalry). During the war the name Jayhawk became associated with courageous fighting and comradeship.

At the end of the war, the university adopted the mythical Jayhawk as part of KU's yell, and in 1912 student Henry Maloy sketched a cartoon Jayhawk that became the first mascot. There have been several changes to that drawing, of course, and in the 1960s the two-dimensional Jayhawk became the three-dimensional "Jay," a costumed mascot.

Mythical birds also lay eggs, it seems, and during the Homecoming game halftime show in 1971 a large one was rolled out to midfield where "Baby Jay" hatched and joined the KU family.

Game-Day Traditions
The Rock Chalk Chant

For more than a century this has been the battle cry for KU football fans (as well as other school sports). It came from a chemistry professor in 1886 who wrote it not to support the football team, but for the Science Club.

That professor was E. H. S. Bailey who, along with some colleagues returning to Lawrence from a conference, used the cadence of their train on the tracks as the inspiration for the chant. The original chant was "Rah, Rah, Jayhawk, K.U.," and the Science Club loved it. However, an English professor had an issue with it. Specifically, with the "Rah, Rah," and he suggested to Bailey he replace it with "Rock Chalk" since it rhymed with Jayhawk and paid tribute to the chalky limestone formations on Mount Oread, where the university sits.

The suggestion was taken, the change made, and it became the official college yell in 1887. Two years later the yell changed again to be chanted in a slow, drawn-out cadence repeated twice and followed by three staccato repetitions. That one was a winner; the Rock Chalk Chant hasn't changed since.

"I'm a Jayhawk"

Talk about the Sooners, the Cowboys and the Buffs,

Talk about the Tiger and his tail,

Talk about the Wildcat, and those Cornhuskin' boys,

But I'm the bird to make 'em weep and wail.

Chorus:

'Cause I'm a Jay, Jay, Jay, Jay Jayhawk

Up at Lawrence on the Kaw

'Cause I'm a Jay, Jay, Jay, Jay Jayhawk

With a sis-boom, hip hoorah.

Got a bill that's big enough to twist the Tiger's tail,

Husk some corn and listen to the Cornhusker's wail,

'Cause I'm a Jay, Jay, Jay, Jay Jayhawk,

Riding on a Kansas gale.

Visiting Kansas

Lawrence was created by a group of abolitionists who came to Kansas shortly after the territory was opened up. Their goal was to keep the state from becoming a slave state. Kansas did choose to be a free state, and that decision was a costly one for Lawrence. In 1856 pro-slavery forces rode into town and burned parts of the city. In 1863 they came back to "burn every house and kill every man." They almost did. They burned most of the city to the ground and killed an estimated 200 men and boys. Of course, the town rebuilt and is now a college town that is home to three universities.

Where to Stay

❶ Eldridge Hotel: The Free State Hotel was built on this site in 1855, but was burned to the ground—twice—by pro-slavery forces. Colonel Eldridge rebuilt the hotel each time, the last time giving his name to the place. It deteriorated over time, and in 1925 the owners tore down the original Eldridge and built the current one. In 2005 it was renovated and is now an all-suite, full-service hotel with a restaurant and bar on-site. Rooms run $119–$179. (*(785) 749-5011, eldridgehotel.com*) ❷ Circle S Guest Ranch & Country Inn: This 1,200-acre ranch, homesteaded in the 1860s, has been in the innkeeper's family for five generations. The home and its 12 rooms have been modernized, but still feature many authentic prairie-life touches. Many of the rooms have whirlpool tubs, fireplaces, and private baths. There are also spa services on-site. Rooms run $155–$245. (*(800) 625-2839, circlesranch.com*) ❸ **Halcyon House Bed & Breakfast:** This 1885 Victorian house is just three blocks from downtown Lawrence and on the northeast edge of the KU campus. There are nine guest rooms with European-inn flair. There is also a Carriage House with a private bath, whirlpool-style tub, and kitchenette. Rooms run $49–$149. The Carriage House will cost you $129–$149. (*(888) 441-0314, thehalcyonhouse.com*) ❹ **Three Sisters Inn:** This restored, turn-of-the-century home is just 15 minutes south of Lawrence. There are four standard bedrooms and one suite, all with private baths. The house and guest rooms are decorated in authentic period style. You will get your choice of a full or Continental breakfast in the morning. Rooms run $149–$99. (*(785) 594-3244, 3sistersinn.com*) ❺ **Clinton State Park:** Located four miles west of Lawrence, the park has 404 sites, 240 of them with hookups. It's a state park, so you have plenty of choices for outdoor recreational activities such as hiking, fishing, and boating. The park has basic amenities and dirt-cheap rates: $7–$8. (*(785) 842-8562, kdwp.state.ks.us/news/state_parks/locations/clinton/camping*)

Where to Eat

TAILGATER SUPPLIES: ❶ **Community Mercantile:** Also known as simply "The Merc," this co-op offers natural and organic foods produced locally. They cut steaks, chops, and chicken every day and grind hamburger almost daily. And if you forgot your cooking utensils at home, they can take care of you, too. (*(785) 843-8544, communitymercantile.com*)

SPORTS BARS: ❷ **Henry T's Bar & Grill:** Henry's is one of those places that has a loyal following of folks who like to hang out on game day. They have 20 TVs and a menu that features some of the largest burgers in town. (*$, (785) 749-2999*) ❸ **JB Stouts Sports Bar & Grill:** Voted "Best Sports Bar" in the 2006 "Best of Lawrence" poll, this is as much a restaurant as a sports bar. The interior is huge, but still manages to feel cozy, despite 27 TVs broadcasting all kinds of sports all the time. The menu is extensive, serving everything from steaks to sandwiches. Several regulation pool tables are available by the hour. Live music on Tuesdays. (*$, (785) 843-0704*)

RESTAURANTS:　❹ **Free State Brewing Company:** Lawrence loves this restaurant like it loves KU sports. Its in-house brews are considered among the best in the Midwest, with six or so $3 pint offerings ranging from a Wheat State Golden to an Oatmeal Stout. The menu is loaded with a dozen-plus local favorites (try the black bean quesadillas, basil ciabatta, or garden burger) in addition to their daily specials. The environment is stylish, busy but friendly. (*$, (785) 843-4555, freestatebrewing.com*) ❺ **Mirth:** This combination coffee shop/Internet café/restaurant offers a cozy atmosphere and several full dinner entrees—fish, steaks, pizzas, sandwiches, veggie options—at reasonable prices. Locals also say it serves one of the better breakfasts in town, available until 4 p.m. (*$, (785) 841-3282*) ❻ **Scarlet Orchid:** If you're looking for a romantic place to have a meal, the Orchid exudes sex-appeal and understated glamour. The dim lighting turns its orange walls a smoky pumpkin and the center dividing wall a deep, mysterious crimson. The décor is otherwise clean-lined and minimalist, contrasting nicely with the menu's highly flavored, fusion-style dishes. Try the tuna tartar salad (ruby-red cubes of seasoned tuna with chunks of avocado) or their fried rice, served in a fresh, hollowed-out pineapple half. (*$, (785) 832-8886, scarletorchid.com*)

❼ **Teller's:** Housed in an old-style bank building, Teller's has the ambience market cornered, with high ceilings, elegant artwork, and hanging milk glass lighting. You can spot vestiges of the restaurant's former life near its restrooms (you walk through a massive bank vault doorway to get to them). The menu's on the upscale side, with a variety of regional Italian specialties, and a strong focus on wines (it

garnered a 2005 *Wine Spectator* Award of Excellence—one of only four places in Kansas and the only one in Lawrence to do so). (*$$, (785) 843-4111, tellerslawrence.com*)

Daytime Fun

❶ **Atchison:** This is a great day trip from Lawrence and is best known as the birthplace of Amelia Earhart. Her grandparents' Victorian home is now the **Amelia Earhart Birthplace Museum** run by the Ninety-Nines, an organization of women pilots the aviator formed in 1929. Also in town is the **International Forest of Friendship**, related to Earhart in the sense it is a living memorial to those involved in aviation and space exploration. There's a park and trees representing the 50 states and 35 countries. And while you're here you may want to keep an eye out for ghosts. They say Atchison is "the Most Haunted Town in Kansas." ❷ **KU Natural History Museum:** This museum is nationally recognized for its public exhibits and collections. Permanent exhibits include fossils of dinosaurs like Annabelle, a 50-foot-long, 140-million-year-old camarasaurus dinosaur. The museum is also home to Comanche—a (stuffed) horse and the only U.S. Army survivor of the Battle at Little Bighorn. With six floors, you'll find plenty to keep you interested. One note: Visitors must use the metered spaces in the garage north of 13th St. at $1 an hour. (*$, (785) 864-4450, nhm.ku.edu*) ❸ **Spencer Museum of Art:** The museum's art collection is comprehensive, spanning European, North American, and East Asian art. Special standouts are their medieval art collection, classical Japanese artwork, and 20th-century Chinese paintings. Frequent independent films make for some unusual viewing. (*Free, (785) 864-4710, ku.edu/~sma/*)

Nighttime Fun

❶ **Abe & Jake's Landing:** Once the site of the Consolidated Barbed Wire Company, Abe & Jake's Landing takes its name from two local fishermen who fished next to the plant back in 1895. A variety of national acts, including Digital Underground, Vanilla Ice, The Wailers, Blues Traveler, Jurassic 5, and G-Love & Special Sauce have rocked sell-out crowds here. With its music and unique multilevel construction, Abe & Jake's was named "Best Overall Bar" by University of Kansas students for 2002. (*$–$$$, (785) 841-5855, abejakes.com*)

❷ **The Bottleneck:** A block east of Massachusetts Street, this tavern draws new bands on the verge of hitting the big time. The music here spans across the genres, from rock and punk to blues and acoustic folk. Some former alums

include Everclear, Widespread Panic, The Foo Fighters, Lucinda Williams, and Jewel. (*$–$$, (785) 842-LIVE, bottlenecklive.com*) ❸ **Liberty Hall**: This combination movie theater and concert hall is a favorite of touring bands and soloists passing through the Midwest. Folks like Guster, Cuban band Los Van Van, and Nashville musicians Bela Fleck and the Flecktones have stood on stage while fans yelled for more. The Hall also shows international, independent, and sometimes just plain fringe-element movies. (*$–$$$, (785) 749-1972, libertyhall.net*)

Shopping

❶ **Blue Dandelion**: Sure, it's basically kids clothing and "stuff" but all done in a really interesting way. You'll find products by area craftspeople and artisans, including handcrafted oak children's furnishings, children's clothing and accessories, and custom bedding. The cabin-style solid cedar beds by Native American artisan Jerry Cruz are particularly impressive. (*(785) 856-8210, bluedandelionkids.com*) ❷ **Diane's Artisan Gallery, Inc.**: This shop doubles as the owner's studio where she weaves shawls, stoles, and scarves on a loom. The gallery also carries top-of-the-line fine crafts by artisans across the country, ranging from glass, wood, pottery, jewelry, and quilts made from recycled sweaters. (*(785) 856-1155, dianesartisangallery.com*) ❸ **Jayhawk Spirit**: Yep, they've got your Jayhawk items. And lots of them. They have a brick and mortar location downtown, but their Internet store sells to a nationwide audience. You'll find everything from sportswear to unusual collectibles. (*(785) 749-5194, jayhawkspirit.com*) ❹ **Massachusetts Street**: This is where the cool shopping is located. Up and down this street are dozens of really neat, fun, and eclectic stores. Included in the mix are antique malls and stores with world and tribal items. ❺ **Riverfront Chocolates**: This gourmet chocolate shop specializes in made-to-order gourmet caramel apples, truffles, fudge, nut clusters, and much more. Since nothing's made in advance, your goodies will be as fresh as humanly possible. (*(785) 749-4211, riverfrontchocolates.com*)

KANSAS STATE

Kansas State University: 23,141 students
Manhattan, KS: pop. 44,831
Bill Snyder Family Football Stadium: seats 50,000
Colors: Purple and White
Nickname: Wildcats
Mascot: Willie
Phone: (800) 221-2287

Reserved RV spots in East and West stadium lots; only Booster Club members can stay overnight before or after. General parking for all vehicles in Lot 9, Chester Peters Recreation Center Lot, or satellite lots surrounding the stadium and other paved campus lots. General parking is $25 for RVs, $10 for cars. No alcohol allowed on campus; no ground fires; no bikes, skateboards, or scooters in parking lots.

Shuttle Info: All parking and tailgating within easy walking distance. No shuttles needed.

Wildcats Media Partners: 1350-AM KMAN, 101.5-FM KMKF

In 1858 the Kansas Territorial legislature incorporated Bluemont Central College in Manhattan. Five years later the new Kansas state legislature founded the Kansas State Agricultural College, which replaced Bluemont and took over the campus (Kansas State moved to its present location in 1875). Perhaps the most historically significant part of this is that Kansas State was the first newly created land-grant college under the Morrill Act. The key words there are *newly created*—there are older land-grant schools that were incorporated from existing colleges.

The school opened with 52 students—evenly divided between men and women. There were the usual philosophical battles between administrators

about whether curriculum should be focused more toward agriculture or liberal arts. Basically, whatever the current university president thought won the battle for his tenure. In 1882 K-State was the first university to offer home economics, part of a growing curriculum that now includes more than 250 degree programs.

During the 20th century the school continued to grow, was renamed Kansas State University (1955), and underwent a lot of construction including new residence halls and a student union. From the mid-1970s to the mid-1980s there was a dip in enrollment and several of the faculty resigned, but a new university president brought donors and students back to campus.

One student who spent his college years in Manhattan was Earl Woods who, in 1951, broke the color barrier in baseball in what was then the Big 7. You probably know him better as Tiger Woods's father.

When Earl Woods was at K-State, he had to endure some pretty bad Wildcat football teams. He wasn't alone. In fact, just about every student who attended the school from 1893—when the first team took the field—until 1989 had to endure pretty bad teams.

With the exception of a few years here and there (those years were mostly in the 1920s and 1930s), K-State had one of the worst teams in college football. But that all changed in 1989.

That was the year Bill Snyder came to Manhattan. The coach turned the Wildcats around, and in his 17 years as head coach (he retired in 2005) he led the Wildcats to 11 consecutive bowl games (1993–2003)—the team had been to only one bowl game in its history pre-Snyder—and 6 top-10 finishes in the AP poll. One of those years, 1998, his Wildcats went 11-0 before losing to Purdue in the Alamo Bowl. That year Snyder was named "National Coach of the Year" and won both the Bear Bryant Award and the Bobby Dodd Foundation Award.

It's rare to find a school where one man took a program from one of the worst in the nation to one of the best. Students and alumni called KSU Stadium "The House that Bill Built." Now it really is his house. In 2005 the university renamed KSU Stadium the Bill Snyder Family Football Stadium.

School Mascot

When K-State first took to the field, its football teams were called the Aggies. But just before the 1915 season, a new coach, John Bender, gave his team a new nickname: the Wildcats. Bender lasted just one season. So did Wildcats.

Z. G. Clevenger took over as head coach, and one of his first tasks was renaming the team the Farmers. Clevenger lasted four seasons. So did Farmers.

When Charles Bachman took over as head coach for the 1920 season he renamed the team the Wildcats, and this time it stuck. In 1922, at Bachman's request, two

alumni, who were veterinarians, donated a live bobcat to serve as the team's mascot. His name was Touchdown, and he was the first of a line of live mascots. For several years Touchdown attended games, but now if you want to see Touchdown IX, you'll have to visit Manhattan's Sunset Zoo.

The mascot you'll see crowd-surfing and doing push-ups after K-State touchdowns is Willie the Wildcat. He first appeared in 1947 in a reddish-brown costume. He's undergone many makeovers in the years since, from looks that range from Mickey Mouse–friendly to mean and intimidating to pumped-up to the current Powercat Willie.

The Powercat look comes from the Powercat logo introduced by Coach Bill Snyder when he took over the football program in 1989. The coach wanted a new look and attitude for his teams. Those teams had success, and the Powercat logo replaced a more cartoonish Wildcat logo that is now rarely used.

Game-Day Traditions
The Wabash Cannonball

It may seem odd, but the "The Wabash Cannonball" is a second fight song for KSU.

The song was written about 1880 and was a hit for country music's The Carter Family and Roy Acuff in the 1930s. But it was a fire in 1969 that brought the folk song about a mythical train to K-State.

It was in the fall of 1969 that a fire destroyed KSU's department of music and everything inside. Not even a piece of sheet music was spared. All that was left of the department was what the music director had in his briefcase. It wasn't much, but it did include sheet music for "The Wabash Cannonball."

That was all the music the band had to play at the next football game, so they played it. A lot. A whole lot. And even after they got new sheet music, they continued to play it, and now it's a Wildcat tradition.

Visiting Kansas State

Manhattan—also known as "The Little Apple"—is both a college town and a military town. In addition to students at Kansas State and two smaller universities, Fort Riley's 15,000 soldiers call the city home. Manhattan is also the home town of Cassandra Peterson, better known as TV horror host Elvira, Mistress of the Dark. That tidbit should win you a trivia contest.

Where to Stay

❶ The Morning Star Bed & Breakfast: This historic property is located, appropriately, in Manhattan's historic downtown neighborhood. There are five spacious guest rooms with private baths; each has a vintage-style bed with down comforters and pillows. Bathrooms have two-person Jacuzzis. The look is very Craftsman style—elegant and homey. Breakfast is always a full meal, with dishes such as

Kansas State
Fight Song

"Wildcat Victory"
Fight you K-State Wildcats.
For Alma Mater fight-fight-fight.
Glory into combat for the Purple and White.
Faithful to our colors, we shall ever be,
Fighting ever fighting for a Wildcat Victory!

blueberry French toast or a Greek omelet. Rooms run $89–$179. (*(785) 587-9703, morningstaronthepark.com*) ❷ Scenic Valley Inn: This real log home, built in 2003, resembles a ski lodge or chalet with huge windows letting in sunlight. It lies 2 miles outside of town, on 20 heavily wooded acres. Scenic Valley offers three guest rooms with private baths; each room has a king-size bed and carries on the log cabin feel. The rooms are large enough to accommodate an extra single or double, if you're traveling with a group. Breakfast, a three-course meal, is served whenever you choose. Rooms are $125 for two people and $25 for each additional person. During KSU football weekends a two-night stay is required. (*(785) 776-6831, scenicvalleyinn.com*) ❸ Shortridge House Bed & Breakfast: In the middle of historic downtown, this Victorian clapboard house has two airy, pleasant guestrooms. Both share a large bath with a Jacuzzi tub. Each also has a small in-room refrigerator with free drinks and snacks. The rooms and house fairly resembles any well-to-do Midwestern home circa 1920s and '30s—a bit of Craftsman, a bit of Victorian, a bit of other, blended into a whole. Rooms are $85 to $110. A two-night stay is required during football weekends. (*(785) 565-0086, shortridgehouse.com*) ❹ Tuttle Creek State Park/River Pond Campground: This newly expanded campground, just a few miles outside town, has 167 sites with water and electric hookups available. Everything here is brand-spanking new and in great shape. A site and vehicle permit (you need both) run $23.50 until October, after which the price drops to $19.50. (*(785) 539-7941, kdwp.state.ks.us/ news/state_parks/locations/tuttle_creek*)

Where to Eat

TAILGATER SUPPLIES: ❶ Downtown Farmers' Market: You can find meats, cheeses, eggs, baked goods, and all kinds of fruits and veggies at this twice-a-week farmers' market until the end of October. On Wednesdays, the market's located north of CiCo Park and Kimball and runs from 4 to 7 p.m. On Saturdays, it moves to the courthouse parking lot at the 400 block of Humboldt and goes from 8 a.m. to 1 p.m. (*(785) 468-3543*) ❷ **People's Grocery Cooperative Exchange:** If you're looking for produce, this could be your place. The food co-op is dedicated to peace, love, and fresh, organic produce. You can also buy cruelty-free bath products and a variety of environmentally friendly items. But you probably won't find meats here, though, or anything made by, or from, animals. (*(785) 539-4811, kansas.net/~organic/*)

SPORTS BARS: ❸ **The Purple Pig:** This fun little K-State sports bar and grill has satellite TVs (seven big screens and seven 24-inch screens) and a full-service kitchen. It's one of the few bars that still allows smoking indoors. Depending on your point of view, that's a blessing or a curse, since the Pig is bit on the smallish side. (*$, (785) 539-7444*)

RESTAURANTS: ❹ **Harry's:** Variously called Harry's Uptown, Harry's Downtown, and Harry's Supper Club, it's all the same restaurant, located in the historic Wareham Hotel Building. It's also probably the Little Apple's fanciest restaurant. The dining room pays homage to its origins with ornate plaster molding, chest-

high wainscoting, and deep-toned wallpaper fencing in numerous dining tables. The menu has a few surprises tucked between more traditional entrées, like its braised fresh bacon—seared pork belly, braised with zinfandel and cognac. The appetizers also show a little inventiveness, with a hot lobster martini and barbecue pork napoleon. (*$$, (785) 537-1300, harrysmanhattan.com*) ❺ **Little Apple Brewing Company:** Called LAB by the locals, this brewery-restaurant crafts some decent beers and serves solid food. The chefs know their steak— it's all USDA Prime or Choice Certified Angus beef. Other LAB entrée options include the local favorite, smothered steak and black bean burrito. The décor here is Midwest clean and simple, with lots of wood and high ceilings. (*$–$$, (785) 539-5500, littleapplebrewery.com*) ❻ **Rock-A-Belly Bar & Deli:** This fun, kitschy diner is located in Aggieville. Inside you'll find enough local retro color to keep your eyes busy for hours. The menu is simple and delicious: sandwiches, salads, and three choices of soup. There's a "No Crybabies" sign on the front door, but well-behaved children are more than welcome (maybe the sign isn't for them, anyway?). By 8 p.m. the liquor begins to flow, and the adults come out to play, as Rock-A-Belly turns into a zippy little nightspot. (*$, (785) 539-8033, rockabellydeli.com*)

Daytime Fun

❶ **Konza Prairie:** This is an 8,600-acre tall grass prairie preserve owned by the Nature Conservancy and Kansas State University. If you thought that prairie meant boring and flat, Konza will show you the error of your ways. It's actually hilly—really, steeply hilly—lush, green, and brimming with wildlife ranging from bison to large-mouth bass. Fourteen miles of nature trails are open to the public from sunrise to sunset daily. (*$, (785) 587-0441, k-state.edu/konza*)

❷ **KSU Insect Zoo:** Occupying a ground-floor space of just more than 1,100-square feet, the Insect Zoo features lots of live insects and their arthropod relatives in naturalistic exhibits. If you call ahead, you can get a guided tour. That's a cool thing to do, because during guided tours visitors can "pet" some of the critters, including millipedes, walking sticks, and tarantulas. (*$, (785) 532-2847, k-state.edu/butterfly*) ❸ **Riley County Historical Museum:** Located in the Riley County Courthouse Plaza, this little museum offers some surprisingly good exhibits exploring the region's Indigenous Peoples (the Kansa Indians), early settlers, and their lifestyles. The museum is open Tuesday through Friday,

8:30 a.m. to 5 p.m., and Saturday and Sunday, 2 to 5 p.m. (*Free, (785) 565-6490, rileycountyks.gov/index.asp?NID=328*)

Nighttime Fun

❶ **Aggieville:** Located southeast of campus, Aggieville started out as a bookstore, barber shop, and a mix of services in 1889. Today it's a five-block mix of restaurants, bars, clubs, more than 100 shops, and all manner of fun stuff. If you're looking for nightlife or want to do a KU-themed pub and club-crawl, this is where your evening should begin, and probably end, too. Aggieville is a favorite with students, and treasured by returning alumni. ❷ **Auntie Mae's:** This started out in 1930 as a speakeasy, run by the plucky widow of a guy who owned a plumbing store. It reopened in 1977 and was named in honor of the resourceful Dora Mae Walters. If you drop by for a visit, be sure to try a tarantula and listen to one of the songs on Auntie Mae's well-stocked jukebox. Auntie Mae's also keeps a full calendar of live music, running the gamut from rock to soul to jazz. (*$, (785) 539-8508, auntiemaes.com*) ❸ **O'Malley's Alley:** This is a must for every Aggieville pub crawl. The Belfast Bomber comes very highly recommended—according to several visitors it's a must try. Game day or not, there's always a good crowd. But remember to carry cash: they don't take plastic. (*$, (785) 537-0775*)

Shopping

❶ **Atomic-Age:** This antique and thrift store specializes in the designs of the 1920s to 1970s, with an emphasis on the 1940s to 1960s. It also has a large, eclectic selection of contemporary products. You can find everything from martini shakers to kitchen tables to lunch boxes. If you're looking to channel your inner lounge lizard, or just get your swank on, this is a good place to spend some time. (*(785) 317-2540, atomic-age.ws*) ❷ **Grand Ol' Trunk Thrift Shop and Bookstore:** This place looks a bit unattractive from the outside, but don't let that fool you— it's much nicer on the inside. The furniture and appliances at Grand Ol' Trunk are bought from estate sales and other venues, but all the clothing has been donated. You literally never know what you'll find. (*(785) 537-2273*) ❸ **Kansas Kollection:** Just like the name suggests, this store is all about anything Kansas, including Kansas State (and even the University of Kansas,

believe it or not). It's also got a big slice of Wizard of Oz collectibles (Dorothy was from Kansas, get it?) and literally anything else associated with the state (tornadoes, wheat, sunflowers, John Deere, etc.). And if you need KSU stuff, look no further—you're already there. (*(785) 539-6900, kansaskollection.com*)

❹ **Varney's Bookstore:** They've got KSU textbooks, KSU clothing, plus loads of KSU gifts and collectibles. You can also find other cool stuff here, like children's books, art supplies, and software. (*(785) 539-8798, varneysbookstore.com*)

MISSOURI

University of Missouri: 21,375 students
Columbia, MO: pop. 90,947
Memorial Stadium: seats 68,345
Colors: Black and Gold
Nickname: Tigers
Mascot: Truman
Phone: (573) 882-7201, (800) CAT-PAWS

RVs park at the Hearnes Center, $50 for weekend. Cars park for $10 in various garages, parking lots, and streets. Tailgaters must stay within their space. No kegs, beer balls, or bulk quantities of alcohol allowed on campus or campus parking areas. Dispose of used coals in specially marked barrels. Note: Childcare available at Pigskin Preschool, located in Child Development Lab at Stanley Hall (nationally recognized childcare facility). Preschool opens 2 hours before game, closes 2 hours after game's end. Children from 6 weeks to 10 years welcome. First child $40, additional siblings $25 each.

Shuttle Info: Courtesy shuttle available from south field level (adjacent to Lot G) to the East and West Gates. Shuttle starts 1 1/2 hours before game, during halftime, and runs until 1 hour after game.

Tigers Media Partners: 1400-AM KFRU, 102.3-FM KBXR

When the University of Missouri was founded in 1839, it was notable for a couple of reasons. For one, it was the first land-grant university west of the Mississippi River. It was also the first university in the Louisiana Purchase territory—a point remembered by Thomas Jefferson's heirs who gave the former president's original tombstone to the university.

Missouri's early years were of steady growth, but then came the Civil War. The war shut down the school for a period while Academic Hall was occupied by Union troops, the president's house used by Federal officers, and

other buildings on campus used for war efforts, including an army hospital.

After the war Missouri resumed classes and began to expand, including the opening of its nationally recognized College of Agriculture.

But in 1892 MU suffered a loss and a challenge. The loss was Academic Hall, which on January 9 was destroyed by a fire some think was caused by the first light bulb west of the Mississippi. The building was a total loss and only the six stone Ionic columns from the front of the building were left standing. They are still standing as Mizzou's most prominent feature at the center of the Red Campus's Francis Quadrangle.

The fire also brought a challenge as several in the state used the disaster as an argument for moving the school to Sedalia. Columbia residents fought back, and Mizzou stayed right where it was. Sedalia got the State Fair.

The 20th century brought growth to MU's programs and student body. In 1908 the world's first school of journalism opened, and it quickly became well-known for its Missouri Method of teaching. It is still considered one of the top J-schools in the world and is the only one to own a commercial newspaper and network-affiliated radio and television stations, which serve as the students' classroom.

After World War II the G.I. Bill brought an influx of students to campus, and the school grew at a rapid pace. This is also the time when Missouri was tagged with its nickname, Mizzou. The school was still called Missouri State University at the time, and the moniker is thought to be the pronunciation of the initials MSU.

Don Faurot was football coach at Mizzou during the postwar boom. He is one of two coaches that highlight MU's football history.

That history began in 1890 when the sophomore class of the Academic School (which is now called the College of Arts and Science) formed Missouri's first team. It was the first of a string of teams that played pretty well, but never became a real power. Mizzou's only bowl game in the pre-Faurot era was the Los Angeles Christmas Festival Bowl in 1924.

But Coach Faurot changed all of that. In 1935 he took over a team that during the three previous seasons combined had managed only two wins. By 1939 he had rebuilt the team and taken it to the Orange Bowl. He would take the Tigers to four more bowl games in his career. Faurot invented the split-T formation and used it to help him amass a 101-79-10 record at Mizzou.

The other coach who gave Tiger fans a lot to cheer about was Dan Devine. In his 13 years as head coach (1958–1970), he led Mizzou to 9 top-20 finishes and 6 bowl games and left MU with a winning percentage (.697) that is still the best of any Missouri head coach.

But it was 1960 that was Devine's most memorable year. The Tigers began the season unranked. But with each win MU inched up in the polls and was undefeated as it played its last game of the season against hated rival the Kansas Jayhawks. A win over KU would seal a national championship. But the Jayhawks stunned the Tigers 23–7. Mizzou won the Orange Bowl but ended the season ranked fifth.

Missouri Fight Song

"Fight, Tiger"

Fight, Tiger, fight for old Mizzou,
Right behind you, everyone is with you.
Break the line and follow down the field,
And, you'll be, on the top, upon the top.
Fight, Tiger, you will always win,
Proudly keep the colors flying skyward.
In the end, we'll win the victory,
So Tiger, fight for Old Mizzou!

"Old Missouri"

Old Missouri, fair Missouri,
Dear old varsity,
Ours are hearts that fondly love thee,
Here's a health to thee.

Chorus:
Proud art thou in classic beauty,
Of thy noble past;
With thy watchwords, Honor, Duty,
Thy high fame shall last.

Every student, man and maiden,
Swells the glad refrain,
Till the breezes music laden,
Waft it back again.

(Chorus)

But the story doesn't end there. It was discovered that Kansas had played an ineligible player and had to forfeit the Missouri game, so the Tigers got the win and a perfect 11-0 season. Nonetheless, only the Poling System poll ranked Missouri number one that year; Minnesota and Mississippi were crowned cochampions by the major polls.

School Mascot

If you think Missouri's Tiger mascot comes from the school colors being black and gold, you're wrong.

It comes from the name of a group of Columbia residents who organized an armed guard and fortified the city against guerilla attacks during the Civil War. They called themselves the Missouri Tigers in hopes the name and fortifications would intimidate the army. Word spread of the Missouri Tigers, and the attacks never came.

So in 1890 when MU fielded a football team and needed a name, they adopted the moniker of these Civil War defenders.

Originally the school had two live tiger mascots—one male, the other female—but neither had a name or could do much to fire up a crowd. So in 1984, to add life to the Tiger, a contest was held to name a mascot. The winning entry was in honor of the Show-Me State's president, Harry Truman, and in 1986 the costumed Truman the Tiger took to the sidelines.

Game-Day Traditions
Homecoming

Although some other schools claim the idea, the NCAA recognizes Mizzou as the birthplace of Homecoming. Missouri is also the answer that gets you points in Trivial Pursuit and on *Jeopardy!*

It happened in 1911 when an NCAA rule change meant all games had to be played on campus. MU and rival Kansas had played their annual game, known as the Border War (now called the Border Showdown), in Kansas City. But with the change the game moved to Columbia that year, and the Tigers' coach was worried attendance would fall because of it. So C. L. Brewer appealed to "Old Grads" to "Come Back Home" for the game. It worked, and the Homecoming tradition was born.

The Missouri Waltz

Written in 1914, and the Missouri state song since 1949, it is game-day tradition for Marching Mizzou to play the Missouri Waltz before and during every home game. The band's version isn't the one you hear from orchestras, though. Its version is a marching-style one.

"Missouri Waltz"

Hush-a-bye, ma baby, slumbertime is comin' soon;
Rest yo' head upon my breast while Mommy hums a tune;
The sandman is callin' where shadows are fallin',
While the soft breezes sigh as in days long gone by.

Way down in Missouri where I heard this melody,
When I was a little child upon my Mommy's knee;
The old folks were hummin'; their banjos were strummin';
So sweet and low.
Strum, strum, strum, strum, strum,
Seems I hear those banjos playin' once again,
Hum, hum, hum, hum, hum,
That same old plaintive strain.
Hear that mournful melody,
It just haunts you the whole day long,
And you wander in dreams back to Dixie, it seems,
When you hear that old time song.
Hush-a-bye, ma baby, go to sleep on Mommy's knee,
Journey back to Dixieland in dreams again with me;
It seems like your Mommy is there once again,
And the old folks were strummin' that same old refrain.
Way down in Missouri where I learned this lullaby,

When the stars were blinkin' and the moon was climbin' high,

Seems I hear voices low, as in days long ago,

Singin' hush-a-bye.

Visiting Missouri

Sometimes called College Town, USA, Columbia is home to not only Mizzou but also to Stephens College and Columbia College. So you can expect to find a town with the charm and activities you would expect in a small college town with almost 35,000 students. Columbia is regularly ranked in national polls as one of the top places to live, and it's also a heath-care center, second only to Rochester, Minnesota, in patient capacity per capita.

Where to Stay

❶ Cottonwoods RV Park: They've got 97 sites with full hookups, including 50-amp electric. There's wireless Internet, but no cable TV or phone hookups. The park's clean and well maintained with level, paved sites that come with picnic tables and chimeneas. Rates are $38. (*(888) 303-3313*) ❷ Guitar Mansion Bed & Breakfast: Built in 1862 by Confederate Army Captain David Guitar, this 4,400-square-foot mansion holds three guest rooms. The B&B is furnished with smooth hardwood floors, period antiques, and an impressive collection of Civil War artifacts. Guest rooms are quite large and impressively decorated in elegant Southern style. Two share a bath, while the third has a private bath. Rooms are $100–$125. (*(573) 814-1860, thequitarhouse.com*) ❸ Stoney Creek Inn: This regional chain (yeah, I'm sort of breaking my "no chain rule" here) is loaded with personality. The lobby (and much of the hotel) is decorated in Yukon-Hunting Lodge style, with log beams, leather and plaid chairs, and other frontier accessories, including a life-sized bear. The inn has 180 rooms and suites available, some tricked-out like log cabins, others slightly more traditional looking; all have free high-speed Internet. During football weekends, rooms run $120–$170, while suites run $205–$300. A two-night stay is required. (*(800) 659-2220, stoneycreekinn.com*) ❹ University Avenue Bed & Breakfast: This B&B is a short walk from Mizzou and has four guest rooms, each with private

baths. Rooms are about the size of a normal bedroom, nicely decorated, with antique bed frames. Breakfast is a full meal, tailored to your dietary needs if advance notice is provided. Rates run $85–$100 and don't change for football games, but some game weekends may require a two-night stay. (*(573) 499-1920, universityavenuebnb.com*)

Where to Eat

TAILGATER SUPPLIES: ❶ **Boone County Farmers' Market:** Local growers sell their fresh produce, meats, eggs, soaps, baked goods, and more here. The market runs until the end of October, Saturdays 9 a.m. to 1 p.m. and Mondays and Wednesdays 4 to 6 p.m. It's located in the rear parking lot of The Marketplace (a group of independent merchants under one roof). (*(573) 443-5009, boonecountyfarmers.com*) ❷ **Columbia Farmers Market:** Fifty-one local vendors sell everything from meats to melons here at this popular open air market. Located on West Ash St., behind the Activity and Recreation Center, the market is open Saturdays from 8 a.m. to 12 noon, and Mondays and Wednesdays 4 to 6 p.m. The market runs until the last Saturday before Thanksgiving. (*(573) 449-GROW, farmersmarket.missouri.org*)

SPORTS BARS: ❸ **Colosseum Bistro:** They claim to be the best of both worlds—restaurant and sports bar. They may be right. With 26 TVs, you'll definitely be able to catch the game. Formerly the Katy Station Restaurant, the atmosphere here is casual and fun—and filled with sports memorabilia. For really concentrated sports-mania, visit the Colosseum's bar, Stumpy Joe Pete's, which has five TVs all to itself. The outdoor patio contains more than 15 tables, and features its own mounted TV so patrons won't miss a second of the game. Hungry sports lovers have a wide array of food choices, from nachos to filet mignon. (*$, (573) 256-2087, colosseumbistro.com*)

RESTAURANTS: ❹ **Flat Branch Pub & Brewing:** They set the standard for microbrewed beer in Columbia and across the state, offering dozens of ales, beers, and ciders brewed on-site. If possible, get a table in the patio out back; it's an oasis of trees and plants. Start out with the artichoke dip (everyone raves about it), then try a slab of their buffalo meatloaf, made with their own oatmeal stout. Save room for a Wild Tiger Float or a Stout Brownie Sundae. Both desserts use stout beer with delicious results. (*$, (573) 499-0400, flatbranch.com*)
❺ **Shakespeare's Pizza:** It's a local legend with the best pizza you'll find within

a 100-mile radius of town. The crust is the right mix of crispy and chewy, with a tasty sauce and the freshest, premium-quality toppings possible. Shakespeare's quirky, silly, take-nothing-but-the-pizza-seriously-attitude is as much fun as the pizza (their ad touting, "We make our own window cleaner" made it onto David Letterman's show several years back). It's been a favorite stop for MU students and alums for over 30 years. (*$, (573) 449-2454, shakespeares.com*)

❻ Sophia's: The closest to a hip, big-city restaurant in Columbia, Sophia's menu is Southern European, with strong Italian influence. It manages to feel both inviting and coolly efficient, with warm earth-colored walls and smoothly polished floors. The outdoor patio has a nearly tropical look. The menu is extensive, with quite a few pizzas and salads listed, as well as a full selection of pastas. Dinner entrées include beef, lamb, chicken, and several fish dishes. Many have a creative twist, like Godiva white chocolate liquor topping a seared, sashimi-grade Ahi tuna. (*$–$$, (573) 874-8009, addisonssophias.com*)

❼ Sparky's Homemade Ice Cream: This is premium ice cream with authentic attitude. On the walls hang various knitted, oddball creatures adopted from thrift shops around the nation. Sparky's ice cream is syrup- and dye-free—such as their peppermint chip ice cream, made with organic peppermint extract, real cream, and Ghirardelli chocolate chunks. The store recently got a liquor license so it can serve "adult" ice cream beverages (although not on Sundays). (*$, (573) 443-7400*)

Daytime Fun

❶ The Activity & Recreation Center: It's raining, you've got kids, and you're wondering how you'll survive; visit the Activity & Recreation Center (ARC). The ARC is a 73,000-square-foot indoor recreation facility with a leisure pool, gymnasium, game room, track, and cardio/strength training zones. The pool has a zero-depth entry, interactive water play feature, triple-loop water slide, lazy river, vortex, three lap lanes, and a heated hydrotherapy pool. Daily passes are available. (*$, (573) 874-7700, gocolumbiamo.com*) ❷ Amish Country at Clark: About 20 miles north of town, this cluster of well-tended Amish farms spreads out for miles. Here you'll see historic farming methods, where fields are still worked with horses and plows, cheek-to-jowl with more modern farming technology. Quilts, molasses, produce, bakery goods, and other items are available at various farms or at the general stores. Tours may be available if you

call ahead. (*$, (573) 682-2272*)

❸ **Museum of Art & Archaeology:** Located in Pickard Hall, this MU museum's permanent collection includes more than 14,000 objects showcasing art ranging from Greek and Roman to American and Byzantium. The museum also hosts rotating, traveling exhibitions. (*Free, (573) 882-3591, maa.missouri.edu*)

❹ **Shryocks Annual Corn Maze:** This annual corn maze covers 12 acres of corn and holds over 4 miles of twisty trails. But these are no ordinary mazes. From the air they take the shape of everything from the MU logo to a map of the United States. The maze starts in mid-July and runs until the end of October and will take at least 1 hour and 15 minutes to get through it, unless you're with a group, in which case it'll take a lot longer. (*$, (573) 592-0191, callawayfarms.com*)

Nighttime Fun

❶ **The Blue Note:** With two full cocktail bars and state-of-the-art sound, light, and video equipment, the Blue Note may be one of mid-Missouri's finest live entertainment venues. Located in a restored vaudeville theater in downtown Columbia, the Blue Note has hosted 20 years worth of up-and-coming artists playing blues, jazz, reggae, alternative/college rock, and folk music. Go and you may see Hank Williams III, the North Mississippi All-Stars, or Better than Ezra, among others. (*$–$$, (573) 874-1944, thebluenote.com*) ❷ **Déjà Vu Comedy**

Club: A good comedy club is a beautiful thing, and this is a good comedy club. The Vu hosts performers such as Tim Allen, Dennis Leary, George Lopez, and Drew Carey, plus the best new names in comedy. There's tiered seating surrounding the stage, giving you a great view no matter where you sit. That's not the only thing that keeps this from being a typical comedy club—more than 65 tons of ventilation equipment with the latest in smoke filtration technology keeps this from being just another smoky club. (*$–$$, (573) 443-3216, dejavucomedy. com*) ❸ **Harpo's:** If you've ever been a student at Mizzou—or visited one—more than likely you've been to Harpo's. This typical college bar has cheap beer, large crowds, and is overflowing with black and gold on game day. (*$, (573) 443-5418*) ❹ **RagTag Cinema:** Fuse a high-minded art-house cinema with a playful, lively beer hall and you have RagTag. They highlight homegrown and far-flung filmmakers, musicians, and performers and hang works by emerging artists on their walls. Don't miss fun events like the True/False Film Festival. (*$, (573) 443-4359, ragtagfilm.com*)

Shopping

❶ The Candy Factory: For more than 30 years, the Candy Factory has been creating and perfecting delicious, gourmet candy recipes. You can sit in their viewing room and watch them make it all, right in front of your hungry eyes. Their rich truffles, fluffy cremes, secret recipe caramels, pecan caramel Katys, and chocolate covered cookies are local favorites, but it's all good. (*(573) 443-8222, thecandyfactory.biz*) **❷ The District:** The District is a stylish shopping area, covering 43 square blocks and bordering MU. With a lively mix of historic architecture, sidewalk cafés, and street musicians, the District is a pretty logical choice for, well, about anything you want. There are more than 110 unique stores, 70 bars and restaurants, and 40 live performances a week happening in various venues. Stores range from clothing boutiques and bookstores to home décor and tattoo parlors. (*(573) 442-6816, discoverthedistrict.com*) **❸ University Bookstore:** It's in the heart of campus, next to Brady Commons, and has everything from the basic Tiger gear and fan supplies to children's cheerleader outfits and steering wheel covers. (*(800) 827-8447, university bookstores.com*)

NEBRASKA

University of Nebraska: 21,792 students
Lincoln, NE: pop. 225,581
Memorial Stadium: seats 81,067
Colors: Scarlet and Cream
Nickname: Cornhuskers
Mascot: Herbie (costumed), Lil' Red (inflatable)
Phone: (402) 472-1800

No RVs on campus, unless members of Booster's clubs. Most campus parking reserved. City offers numerous parking garages with pre-paid, reserved spots for $6–$11. Best bet for tailgaters are lots near state fairgrounds on north side of campus for $5–$10. Largest unreserved campus lots located at Bio Science Greenhouses, between Vine and R Streets. RVers should park rigs in nearby RV parks: Lancaster Event Center, Lincoln's Camp-A-Way, and State Fairgrounds. When tailgating, remember Lincoln's open container laws and other city ordinances. Note: Childcare available for kids 2–12 years old at Jr. Blackshirts Day Camp, in Campus Recreation Center. Camp opens 90 minutes before game, closes 45 minutes after game's end. You MUST preregister for camp; $20 per child.

Shuttle Info: Big Red Express service stops at seven locations around town, $8 round trip. You'll need exact change.

Cornhuskers Media Partners: 1400-AM KLIN, 1110-AM KFAB

When the University of Nebraska opened its doors in 1871, there were just 20 students (although another 110 were in the preparatory school on campus). It was a small campus set up a few blocks from the state capitol anchored by University Hall, which was built from wood and sun-dried bricks. That construction began to crumble by 1886 when the second campus building was erected.

The campus in Lincoln grew and so did the university's mission. In 1873 it opened a farm campus east of town, which in turn grew to outposts around the state.

By 1915 NU had grown so much that there was a heated argument in the state legislature about consolidating the university on the farm campus. The legislature couldn't settle it so a vote of the people did: no consolidation. That led to a rapid building boom on the Lincoln campus and more growth during the next several decades. In fact, in the 10-year period from 1959 to 1969, enrollment jumped from 8,000 to 20,000. That led to more buildings and more growth.

But across America it isn't the academics or campus growth that people know about Nebraska. It's the football.

Since it's first game in 1890 (a 10–0 victory over the Omaha YMCA), it has won far more games than it's lost. The Cornhuskers rank sixth in the nation of the winningest programs of all time. They own nearly 50 conference titles, 5 national titles, and 3 Cornhuskers have won the Heisman Trophy: Johnny Rogers (1972), Mike Rozier (1983), and Eric Crouch (2001).

Along with several star players a couple of star coaches led Nebraska to national prominence.

Bob Devaney coached the Cornhuskers from 1962 to 1972, leading his teams to eight conference titles, nine bowl appearances, and back-to-back national championships in 1970 and 1971. He left Nebraska with 101 wins and an .829 winning percentage—the best in school history. You wouldn't have been criticized for thinking Devaney would go down as the winningest Nebraska coach of all time. But he's not.

The coach to follow him was a guy named Tom Osborne, who in his 25 years leading the Cornhuskers would win 255 games and retire with a winning percentage of .836, which is the fifth best percentage in college football history. He also won 13 conference championships and 3 national championships (1994, 1995, and 1997), and came close a few other times.

School Mascot

During the 19th century Nebraska's teams were called everything from the Old Gold Knights to the Rattlesnake Boys to the Bugeaters. It was that last moniker the team held in 1899 when Lincoln sportswriter Cy Sherman (who later would help originate the AP poll) decided he'd had enough of the unflattering name.

Iowa's football team had been called the Cornhuskers from time to time, and Cy liked the name. Since Iowa had decided to go with Hawkeyes as its nickname, Cy figured Cornhuskers was available and started calling Nebraska's team that in

1900. Fans and administrators agreed with him and the name stuck. Legislators did, too, later making it the official nickname for the state.

There wasn't any official mascot or symbol for the Cornhuskers, so over the years several cartoonists and illustrators created some. None generated any excitement until 1974 when a Texan created Herbie Husker.

That Texan was artist Kirk West of Lubbock who sketched the cartoon for the Cotton Bowl press headquarters (NU played in the Cotton Bowl that year). Nebraska's Sports Information director saw it, liked it, and Herbie's been the Cornhusker ever since.

He's gone through some changes over the years—both in illustration and in costume. Most recently in 2003 the costumed Herbie traded his denim coveralls, red cowboy hat with an "N" on the front, and an ear of corn in his pocket for the more updated look of blue jeans, red work shirt, red cowboy hat, and work boots.

Herbie also has a friend, Lil' Red, an inflatable mascot that entertains the crowd by bouncing and dancing around the sidelines.

And one quick note in case you want to pull a Cy Sherman and use Bugeaters for your school's mascot since Nebraska isn't using it anymore, the school's a step ahead of you. It's still a registered trademark for the university. Sorry.

Game-Day Traditions
Tunnel Walk

On game-day Saturdays Memorial Stadium becomes the third largest city in Nebraska. And most every one of the 81,000 fans is standing and cheering as the team lines up in the tunnel to take the field. But before the team runs from the tunnel, the scoreboard lights up with computer animation, and the Alan

Parsons Project's "Sirius" blares from the PA system. Then, as the energy reaches its peak, the team emerges ready to take on another opponent. They've been entering the field this way to sold-out crowds since 1994.

Blackshirts

This is the name that's become a common nickname for the Nebraska defense. It's a tradition that dates back to the 1960s when coach Bob Devaney decided to give his defense contrasting practice jerseys from the offense's red ones. The shirts that an assistant coach chose were black, and they began calling the defensive unit the Blackshirts. But not everyone on defense is a Blackshirt.

It's just the first unit that gets to wear the jerseys. Until recently you found out if you were a Blackshirt at the beginning of the week by finding one hanging in your locker. Now there's a team ceremony to hand them out to defensive starters. Before bowl games all senior defensive players are awarded honorary Blackshirts to wear before the game.

Visiting Nebraska

Lincoln is named for President Abraham Lincoln, but it wasn't to honor him as much as it was a political ploy by Omaha politicians to get the state capital. The Nebraska Territory capital had been in Omaha, but much of the population had moved south of the Platte River, and there was talk of Kansas annexing those areas. So Nebraska decided to move the capital south of the river and westward to the village of Lancaster. To stop the move the Omaha loyalists had Lancaster's name changed to Lincoln—the thought being the move wouldn't happen if the city were named Lincoln due to the

ALMA MATER

"Dear Old Nebraska U"
("No Place Like Nebraska")

There is no place like Nebraska,
Dear old Nebraska U.
Where the girls are the fairest,
The boys are the squarest,
Of any old school that I knew.
There is no place like Nebraska,
Where they're all true blue.
We'll all stick together,
In all kinds of weather,
For Dear old Nebraska U!

Confederate sympathies of the state. It didn't work, and Lincoln became the state capital when Nebraska was admitted to the Union in 1867.

Where to Stay

❶ **Anniversary Mansion Bed & Breakfast:** A Neoclassical mansion, it specializes in getaways for married couples, but sports fans are welcome, too. This B&B has three suites, each furnished with a plush king-size bed. The private baths are decked out with whirlpools or Jacuzzis. This place is posh, without feeling intimidating or awkward. Guests get a full breakfast served on the good china, with silver and Waterford crystal in the dining room. Rates are $149–$179. (*(877) 907-4900, bbonline.com/ne/anniversary/index.html*)

❷ **Atwood House Bed & Breakfast:** Another Neoclassical mansion just two blocks from Nebraska's capitol. All suites have private baths, and all but one have Jacuzzi or whirlpool tubs. You'll also get monogrammed towels and robes. It's a pretty ritzy looking place, but not too frilly, with lots of white marble in the bathrooms and some very ornate antique beds. Their full breakfast (served on bone china, with sterling silver and Waterford crystal) can be sent to your room, if you wish. Suites run $115–$199. (*(800) 884-6554, atwoodhouse.com*)

❸ Camp-A-Way: Located in Lincoln, there are 91 sites here with full hookups. You also get phone and cable TV hookups and Internet service. Sites are large and shady. The park's grounds and facilities are well maintained. During football weekends, sites run $29–$36 (normal rates) but require a two-night stay. You can also rent a site and an RV for $65, with a two-night stay. The park runs a "Huskers Home Game Season Special" where fans can park their RV for five weeks at a discounted price. (*(866) 719-2267, campaway.com*) **❹ The Cornhusker Hotel:** Okay, this is totally a Marriott hotel and breaks my rule, but it's named The Cornhusker, and that's worth something. This 10-story landmark hotel comes complete with a grand, spiral staircase and lavishly hand-painted murals (you don't find that in your average Marriott). It's a first-rate, four-star hotel with 297 newly renovated rooms, plus 12 suites. Most rooms run $239 during football season; reserve early. (*(888) 236-2427, thecornhusker.com*)

Where to Eat

TAILGATER SUPPLIES: **❶ Haymaker's Farmers' Market:** Located in the historic Haymarket District, it's open every Saturday from 8 a.m. to 12 noon, until mid-October. You'll find loads of locally grown produce, meats, eggs, and handmade

arts and crafts. If you've had a hankering for elk or buffalo, you'll find it here. There's live music and other entertainment as well. (*(402) 435-7496, historichaymarket.info*)

SPORTS BARS: ❷ **Cappy's Hotspot Bar & Grill:** A more recent addition to Lincoln's bar scene, Cappy's has become a popular spot for local sports lovers. The plasma TVs are the first thing to catch your eye. There are several on the main dining room's walls, ensuring a good view no matter where you sit. The menu has an extensive choice of burgers, sandwiches, appetizers, and entrées. Try the fried ravioli to start, then dive into one of Cappy's burgers. (*$, (402) 421-1424, cappysbar.com*) ❸ **The N Zone:** This fun sports pub serves pizza and chicken wings to fans while they watch the Huskers on one of the bar's 17 TVs. Three of those are (really) big-screen jobs. For the restless customer, there's pool, foosball, darts, and video golf to play. The Zone has a mural across its back wall celebrating Nebraska sports and jerseys from some of football's greats, such as Dan Marino and John Elway. (*$, (402) 475-8683, the-n-zone.com*)

RESTAURANTS: ❹ **Blue Orchid Thai Restaurant:** This elegant, upscale restaurant serves beautifully cooked and arranged Thai food. The interior features a five-tone green color scheme, with handmade textiles and 100-year-old bells from Thailand. The menu features dishes created from favorite family recipes—the two owners' (a professor and his restaurateur wife) are often joined in the kitchen by their mothers, who help cook. Try the Orchid chicken, served in a hollowed out pineapple-half. (*$, (402) 742-7250*) ❺ **Dish:** If you're looking for top-shelf dining that you don't have to scalp your game tickets to afford, you'll want to try Dish. The menu owes a lot to French bistro food, but also borrows from Korea, India, and South America. The result is dishes like moqueca, a Brazilian seafood stew, Argentinean-style flank steak, and Korean barbecue salmon. Inside, the restaurant's got a pretty bold, spare look—red walls, black floor, and yellow accents. (*$$, (402) 475-9475, dishdowntown.com*) ❻ **Scrumpy Jack's:** Nestled into a back corner of a bland strip mall, its oversized door tells you this isn't an ordinary chain restaurant. Inside, you'll find a warm and stylish place with curving lines, warm colors and lighting. The menu is big on steaks and seafood (salmon, scallops, walleye, tuna). The sesame tuna with wakame salad, and the jumbo scallops with mushroom risotto are favorites. (*$–$$, (402) 434-6061, scrumpy jacks.com*)

Daytime Fun

❶ Great Plains Art Museum: The museum houses an impressive collection of Western art, featuring bronzes by Frederic Remington, works on paper by Albert Bierstadt, and other artists and photographers of the American West and Great Plains. The gallery's changing exhibitions focus on significant regional art, including paintings by 20th-century American Indian artists. This is art that will catch your eye and hold it. (*Free, (402) 472-6220, unl.edu/plains/gallery/*

gallery.html) ❷ **James Arthur Vineyards:** Northwest of Lincoln, this vineyard is one of the best wineries in the state and loves visitors. While visiting, guests can enjoy specialty wines, cheeses, meats, and breads in the tasting room, complete with a stone fireplace and an observation deck overlooking the production facility or outside (weather permitting). Weekend vineyard tours are available. The facility is handicapped accessible and offers wine and related products for sale. (*Free, (402) 783-5255, jamesarthurvineyards.com*)

❸ **Pioneers Park:** This 1,100-acre park has lots of artwork, an outdoor amphitheater, picnic areas, hiking and biking trails, ponds, a sled run, and a golf course. That can fill up your day. At the west end of the park is a 668-acre Nature Center featuring 8 miles of hiking trails that wind along ponds, past tall-grass prairie, woodlands and wetlands, and across a stream. Along the way, you can expect to see herds of bison, elk, and deer roaming. Non-releasable raptors are on exhibit and prairie, herb, bird, and butterfly gardens bloom (well, depending on when you visit). (*Free, (402) 441-7895, lincoln.ne.gov/city/ parks/nature/ natcenter/index.htm*)

Nighttime Fun

❶ Coyote Willy's: This happy, rowdy bar features themed nights, live bands, a packed dance floor, pool tables, karaoke, and DJs. Try to catch the very popular Twisted Thursdays when guys take turns dancing on top of the bar for cash and prizes. It's a young crowd, but you expected that. (*$, (402) 474-9459, coyotewillys.com*) ❷ Buzzard Billy's: This dependable bar is located in a historic building in downtown Lincoln. It has a large, covered outdoor patio and is walking distance from Memorial Stadium. They also have a pretty good kitchen serving an extensive Cajun-Creole style menu that's several steps up from pub grub. (*$, (402) 475-8822, buzzardbillys.com/nebraska.html*) ❸ Haymarket/Downtown: This former warehouse district is now home to more restaurants, clubs, and bars than you can count. Well, you could count them, but you won't hit them all in one night. From college hangouts to live music to dance clubs, they're all here. (*(402) 434-6900, downtownlincoln.org*)

Shopping

❶ Eyes of the World Imports: Places like this are perfect for finding really cool stuff. Your inner world-beat hippie will love these unique gift and home items,

including Lincoln's largest selection of sterling silver jewelry, lamps, candles, and holders. You'll also find wrought iron garden accents, planters, chimes, and other handmade home decor items from around the world. Some items are a steal; others are pricey. (*(402) 474-0211, eyesoftheworldimports.com*)

❷ **Haymarket/Downtown:** This lively, former warehouse district is full of more than restaurants, clubs, and nightspots. It's also home to scores of unique specialty shops housed in carefully renovated buildings from Lincoln's earlier days. Shopping attractions include antiques and art galleries in the Haymarket building itself, plus a slew of other things in the downtown core. The area stretches from 7th to 15th Streets, and N to R Streets. (*(402) 434-6900, downtownlincoln.org*) ❸ **Huskers Authentic:** Here's the official team store of the Nebraska Cornhuskers. They've got Adidas apparel, autographed memorabilia, team posters, and all the other Husker stuff you'd expect. They're located right across the street from Memorial Stadium. (*(800) 824-4733*) ❹ **Lee Booksellers:** Since 1979, this has been one of Lincoln's best places for books. This service-oriented independent bookstore will gift-wrap and mail your books for free and special orders volumes for anyone who can't find what they're searching for. But, considering Lee's large inventory of books, audio books, magazines, stationery, maps, and items, they'll probably find it. (*(402) 420-1919, leebooksellers.com*) ❺ **Nebraska Bookstore:** This is a bookstore with attitude—Husker attitude. They've got a frighteningly large inventory of Husker clothing, gifts, souvenirs, and books. You could almost furnish your den or TV room from their supply of swag. The upper level contains textbooks if you need one. (*(800) 627-0047, nebraskabookstore.com*)

OKLAHOMA

University of Oklahoma: 28,954 students
Norman, OK: pop. 99,197
Gaylord Family – Oklahoma Memorial Stadium:
   seats 50,000
Colors: Crimson and Cream
Nickname: Sooners
Mascot: Sooner Schooner
Phone: (405) 325-4666

Visiting RVs park at Lloyd Noble Center. The center has 130 spaces with hookups at $80 per weekend, 88 spaces without hookups at $30 per weekend. RVs start arriving as early as 5 p.m. Friday. Tailgating starts 7 a.m. game day, running until kickoff. No tailgating during the game. Open container policy strictly enforced. No pets allowed.

Shuttle Info: Shuttle runs from Lloyd Noble Center to Stadium, $2.

Sooners Media Partner: 1520-AM KOKC

In 1890, 17 years before Oklahoma would become a state, the Oklahoma Territorial legislature formed two public universities. One was in Norman, the other in Stillwater. The first students enrolled at the Norman Territorial University in 1892 and—since the territory apparently needed a lot of pharmacists at the time—the School of Pharmacy became the first specialty in 1893.

   The university's first building was also built in 1893. It was the school's only building when it burned to the ground in 1903. Several other towns used the fire as an argument for the territory to move the school. University president David Boyd, however, immediately began rebuilding and planning for the future campus, saying to detractors, "What do you need to keep classes going? Two yards of blackboard and a box of chalk." The school had that, and it stayed in Norman.

In 1907 the Norman Territorial University became the University of Oklahoma as the territory joined the Union and became a state. The biggest challenge at OU then wasn't academics as much as it was religion. Factions of Presbyterians and Baptists feuded with the Southern Baptists and Methodist factions at the university. The tussles created a lot of turnover, including President Boyd, who lost his job.

But that challenge was overcome, and OU flourished in the early 20th century, growing to 167 acres and nearly 7,000 students by World War II. By the turn of the next century OU had grown to include satellite campuses across the state and about 30,000 students.

It also had grown into the football program with the best winning percentage of any college in the country since the AP poll began in 1936. They've scored more points than any other Division I-A team, produced four Heisman Trophy winners (Billy Vessels in 1952, Steve Owens in 1969, Billy Sims in 1978, and Jason White in 2003), and won seven national championships (1950, 1955, 1956, 1974, 1975, 1985, and 2000).

All of this began in 1895 when John Harts, a student from Kansas, organized a team to play the game he'd played at home. The team was mostly comprised of nonstudents from the area. They weren't very good.

In fact, the first game was a disaster. OU lost to Oklahoma City Town Team 34–0, couldn't even make a first down, and had so many injuries they had to borrow players from the Oklahoma City team just to finish the game.

During the next 10 years, the team got better, but they got *a lot* better in 1905 when Bennie Owen came to campus. Owen coached for 22 seasons, many of them using the forward pass, which was not a popular play yet. It worked for him. He left OU with a 122-54-16 record.

Over the next 20 years, the Sooners had six coaches. But in 1947 Bud Wilkinson came to Norman and turned Oklahoma into a true national power. In his 17 seasons he led the Sooners to a record-setting 47-game winning streak, 14 conference championships, and 3 national championships. During his tenure Wilkinson amassed a 145-29-4 record.

Those numbers wouldn't be matched again at OU until the 1970s and 1980s when Barry Switzer led the Sooners to 12 conference championships, 3 more national championships, and a 157-29-4 record. Although he left OU under a shadow of contro-

ALMA MATER

"Oklahoma, Hail!"

From the hillsides, from the prairies,
Comes a song that never wearies
Loyalty that never varies.
Oklahoma, hail!

Ivied walls and stately towers,
Campus fair 'neath sun or showers,
All the love we bear thee flowers
And will never fail.

Chorus:

Shout the chorus loudly
Bear the emblem proudly
Army vast, we march at last
And lift our voices stoutly.

On we march for Alma Mater,
On we march nor ever falter
Singing loud, each son and daughter,
Oklahoma, hail!

From the gracious font of learning,
We will quench our thirst so burning
Kindly Mother to thee turning.
Oklahoma, hail!

Wisdom brought from out the ages,
Truths of saints and laws of sages
Ours to take from glitt'ring pages,
Never growing stale.

(Chorus)

versy, his version of the Wishbone offense created one of the most powerful offenses college football has ever seen.

School Mascot

The Land Run of 1889 opened up the Oklahoma Territory for settlement. The deal was that anyone could claim a lot of land, but everyone had to start the scramble at the same time. Most did. Some didn't, sneaking into the territory too soon. They had a name for those people: Sooners.

Oklahoma became the Sooner State, and OU became the Sooners in 1908, although the school nickname was taken from a university pep club called the Sooner Rooters. Sooners replaced Rough Riders and Boomers, OU's previous team names.

Those settlers who headed west did so in covered wagons called Conestoga wagons. That's why you see a scaled replica being pulled around the stadium before the game and every time OU scores. It's called the Sooner Schooner, and the white horses pulling it are Boomer and Sooner. The Sooner Schooner was first driven onto the field in 1964 but didn't become the school's official mascot until 1980.

It was the only mascot until 2005 when its costumed cousins were introduced. The school and students wanted a mascot that could mingle with fans, generate excitement, and represent OU at events and other athletic games where horses and a covered wagon wouldn't work. So Boomer and Sooner were created to fill the void. In addition to their regular outfits, the mascots dress in team uniforms for football games.

Game-Day Traditions
Sooner Schooner

The scaled replica of a Conestoga wagon being pulled on the field by the horses Boomer and Sooner after every OU score is one of the nation's best-known traditions. It began in 1964 when the all-male spirit group RUF/NEKS first drove it across old Owen Field.

It is still maintained and driven by the group and makes its famous arc to midfield after every Sooner score. The RUF/NEKS Queen sits next to the driver, and a club member hangs off the back waving the OU flag. It is a tradition that brings Sooner fans to their feet in cheers. It also may have cost OU the 1985 Orange Bowl.

During the third quarter of that game against the Washington Huskies, OU kicked a field goal to break a 14–14 tie, and the Sooner Schooner took to the field for its celebration ride. The problem was the kick was nullified by a penalty. By the time anyone realized that, the Sooner Schooner was in front of the Washington bench and stuck in a wet patch of turf. It finally worked its way out and off the field but not fast enough for the referees who penalized OU for taunting. The penalties meant a 22-yard kick became a 42-yard kick, which the Sooners missed. They lost the game 28–17.

"Boomer Sooner!"

It's one of America's most recognized fight songs, and it was stolen. Okay, not stolen (unless it's a Yale grad telling you the story).

"Boomer Sooner!" came from the pen of student Arthur Alden in 1905. He took the tune to Yale's fight song, "Boola Boola," and reworked the lyrics. It caught on quickly, but some students made an addition the following year, this time borrowing and reworking a line from North Carolina's "I'm a Tarheel Born" to finish out the lyrics that students and alumni sing today. It has become recognized first as Oklahoma's fight song. That's what seven national championships and playing your fight song on national TV every week gets you. (Sorry, Yale.)

Visiting Oklahoma

Norman is a suburb of Oklahoma City (which is about 20 minutes north of campus) and is in many ways a college town, but it is also the nation's meteorology hub. Within the National Weather Center are a number of National Oceanic and Atmospheric Administration (NOAA) organizations and OU's nationally recognized meteorology department. And that Doppler radar you watch on your local TV news every night to know what to wear tomorrow . . . it was invented here.

Where to Stay

❶ A-AAA Adult RV Park: This is a pretty basic RV park with 85 sites with full utility hookups. Lots are level and super-wide, there are laundry facilities, and park owners run a tight ship. While wireless Internet is available, there's no cable TV or phone hookup. The park also lacks showering facilities. Sites are $24. RV club members and senior citizens get a 50 percent daily discount after the first day, even during football weekends. (*(405) 387-3334, a-aaarvpark.com*)

❷ Holmberg House: Location is everything, and this B&B has a good one—right across the street from OU. This Craftsman-style house has four attractive guestrooms, each with a private bath. Two have whirlpool tubs. The décor is relatively true to the Arts and Crafts style; it's comfortable, simple, but never boring. Rooms run $99–$129, with a two-night stay required on football weekends. (*(877) 621-6221, holmberghouse.com*) **❸ Montford Inn:** This two-story home near historic downtown has 10 guest rooms and 6 cottage suites, all with private baths, fireplaces, and Internet connections. Some rooms also feature whirlpool tubs or private hot tubs. Rooms and cottages are attractive and decorated to reflect Oklahoma's history and people, with some sports and OU

memorabilia thrown in. It's a B&B, so you get a breakfast and evening refreshments. Rates run $95–$169 for rooms, $199–$229 for cottage suites. During football weekends a two-night stay is required. (*(800) 321-8969 montfordinn.com*) ❹ **The Sooner Hotel & Suites:** Welcome to Soonerville. Located on campus, this hotel offers guest rooms and suites (but the name gave that away). Guest rooms have twin beds while the suites have two bedrooms with two queen beds. A swimming pool and gym facility are on-site for guests to enjoy. During football season rates for rooms run $59.50, while suites are $119. Both require a two-night minimum stay. (*(888) 777-0477, housing.ou.edu/content/blogcategory/26/160*) ❺ Sooner Legends Inn & **Suites:** This new, boutique-style hotel has all the stuff you'd expect at a new hotel. But did you notice the word "legends"? Each guest room is individually decorated to reflect a former Oklahoma Sooner player, coach, team, or sport. The hotel contains more than 2,000 pieces of Sooner memorabilia. In addition to Sooner stuff, rooms and suites also have granite sinks and vanities, and leather furniture. Rates range from $159 to $279, with a two-night minimum during football weekends. (*(405) 701-8100, soonerlegends.com*) ❻ Whispering Pines

Bed & Breakfast: You'll find seven guest suites (one's a cottage) with private baths here. Located 10 minutes from campus, the atmosphere in five of the guestrooms is very romantic; the remaining two have, respectively, an English hunt or mountain cabin feeling to them. All are large and very well furnished— each bath is equipped with either a whirlpool tub or Jacuzzi. The Whispering Pines also has a French restaurant on its ground floor. Rooms are $100–$185. (*(405) 447-0202, bbonline.com/ok/whisperingpines/index.html*)

Where to Eat

TAILGATER SUPPLIES: ❶ **Forward Foods:** They've been around only since September 2006, but these guys have become popular quickly. Located in downtown Norman, they offer a selection of more than 200 cheeses, organic and fair-trade coffee, and a wide array of specialty foods from around the world. They also have organic produce and artisan breads. The owners, Suzy Thompson and Steve Reynolds, are OU alums and husband and wife. Interesting fact: The business was financed by Steve's winnings from the *Jeopardy!* TV game show in 2003. (*(405) 321-1007, forwardfoods.com*)

❷ **Norman Farmers' Market:** Oklahoma's oldest farmers' market is open every Saturday and Wednesday through October. You can buy fresh seasonal produce, honey, wine and table grapes, potted plants, hanging baskets, cut flowers, trees, shrubs, tropical plants,

and other stuff for your tailgate. (*(405) 360-4721, clevelandcountyfair.org/Farm%20Market.htm*)

SPORTS BARS: ❸ **Coach's:** You're not going to find a more authentic OU sports bar than this one—it's owned by former Oklahoma running back Steve Owens (and some others). You'll find plenty of sports memorabilia here including the 1969 Heisman Trophy Owens won. If you're at Coach's to watch the game, you can pick from about 40 TVs and a large video wall. If you're not there for the game, the billiard room has 18 pool tables. Food-wise, Coach's is known for its menu of hickory-smoked meats, pizzas, salads, and sandwiches, and a large selection of beers brewed on-site. (*$, (405) 360-5726, coachsok.com*) ❹ **The Mont:** Within walking distance of campus, The Mont's been open since 1976, continuing the legacy of an old Norman favorite, the Monterrey restaurant (called "the Mont" by locals). This Mont is the current home of the "Town Tavern" OU football scoreboards, dating back to 1947. They're on display throughout the restaurant, and updated after every OU football game. The kitchen serves Mexican specialties, plus burgers, sandwiches, soups and salads, and specials like chicken-fried steak and chicken. Its patio, a lush, landscaped oasis, has a misting system to keep customers cool during hot Oklahoma weather. (*$, (405) 329-3330, themont.com*) ❺ **The Vista:** For serious Sooner fans this is the place, with more than 40 TVs and 7 big screens. Located a short distance from the stadium, they have a huge video selection of past OU games you can watch, plus plenty of present-time sporting events on TV, much of it in HD. Since the bar's on the sixth floor of an office tower, you'll have an excellent view of the OU campus. (*$, (405) 447-0909, vistasportsgrill.com*)

RESTAURANTS: ❻ **The Diner:** Located in downtown Norman, it's everything a small-town diner should be, with a long, narrow dining room, a counter with swivel stools, worn Formica tabletops, good, friendly service, and a great breakfast. The menu states, "Continuing 100 years of service," and they've got it down to a science. Get the three-egg omelet, then add bacon, ham, or sausage—you'll be out all of $6. The lunch menu features burgers and sandwiches, plus burritos, quesadillas, chili, and soup. Don't stop in for dinner; they close up after lunch. (*$, (405) 329-6642*) ❼ **Gaijin Sushi:** This tiny Japanese restaurant serves sushi, noodles, salads, and soups. The chef knows how to combine the best of East and West for a taste that's true to its Japanese origins, but is more than the same old roll of rice and fish. Japanese food can be

surprisingly kid-friendly—ask your server or the chef for some pointers. (*$, (405) 307-8744*) ❽ **Legends:** This restaurant has been a part of Norman life since 1968, when it started out as a pizza parlor. There's far more than pizza here today. The intimate dining room is filled with original artwork and features a broad menu of pastas, steaks, and daily seafood specials. Try the bleu cheese tournedos of beef for a rich, hearty taste; for a lighter touch, try the salmon with maple-soy glaze. Although the menu says "fine dining," the atmosphere is rather casual. (*$$, (405) 329-8888, legendsrestaurant.com*) ❾ **Misal Bistro:** Like something out of a Rudyard Kipling book, this Indian restaurant's interior is impressive, with hand-enameled flowers, colorful shamianas, an interior courtyard, and hand-carved figures from Hindu mythology. The cuisine is equally fine with seven kinds of breads, like naan, cooked in a clay oven, or papar, a spicy lentil wafer. Vegetarians will love Misal's Navrathan platter. Omnivores should try the Tandoori sampler. If you want something more creative, go for the Orange Zest Salmon, or the rack of lamb seasoned with saffron, cardamom, basil, and rosemary. Be sure to make reservations. (*$–$$, (405) 579-5601, misalofindia.net*)

Daytime Fun

❶ Canadian River Winery: You didn't know the Sooner State had a wine industry, did you? Just south of Norman the Canadian River Winery has a 7-acre vineyard where it produces several wines—all of which you can taste on a tour. A large assortment of Oklahoma cheeses are also on hand. The Canadian River is just one of several wineries in the region, so log on to OklahomaWines.org to learn about and visit some others. (*$, (405) 872-5565, canadianriverwinery.com*)

❷ Casinos: You don't have to drive to Vegas to get in a little blackjack. There are two casinos nearby, the **Thunderbird Casino** and the new **Riverwind Casino**. The Thunderbird has a Wild West town straight out of the 1880s surrounding it. The Riverwind has a more modern style, with performers appearing nightly. (*$–$$$, Thunderbird Casino (405) 360-9270, Riverwind Casino (405) 322-6000, riverwind.com*) **❸ The Jacobson House:** This unique museum is named after its original owner, Oscar B. Jacobson. He served as the first director of the OU's School of Art, mentoring and promoting the famous "Kiowa Five" Indian Artists. Their success initiated a renaissance of Indian painting on the Plains, known as the Oklahoma School of Traditional Painting, which still influences Native American art today. The house became a museum in the late

1980s and still functions as an important center of Native American culture, with exhibits, classes, poetry readings, and art demonstrations open to the public. (*Free, (405) 366-1667, jacobsonhouse.com*)

❹ **Little River Zoo:** If you've seen those mega-zoos, be prepared for a more personalized experience. The emphasis here is on a nontraditional, humane, educational experience. At this 55-acre zoo, every visitor receives a personally guided tour, giving you not just facts about the animals but who they are, where they came from, and the differences in their personalities. Who knew Ellie, the Fennec Fox, gets jealous of all the attention Moby, the South American Coati, gets? Or that Blossom, a North American Black Bear, is really a little shy with strangers? (*$, (405) 366-7229, littleriverzoo.com*)

Nighttime Fun

❶ **Bricktown Entertainment District:** If you want to stay up all night and party until the sun rises, this is your destination. Located up the road in Oklahoma City, this is an entire district devoted to restaurants, nightclubs, live music, dancing, and (during the day) shopping. Catch the yellow **Bricktown Water Taxi**, on the Bricktown Canal for a relaxing, 1-mile ride. While you're here, stop into Toby Keith's **I Love This Place Bar & Grill** to see more than 100 pieces of Toby Keith memorabilia, or slink into **SKKY Bar Ultra Lounge** to experience its state-of-the-art sound and light system and an easy-to-love menu of dance remixes from the '70s, '80s, and '90s. ❷ **Citywalk:** In the heart of Bricktown, this unique destination holds nine clubs and bars under one roof, Thursday through Saturday nights. Step into **Dirty Martini** for an upscale atmosphere and a stiff drink. **City Limits** is a 10,000-square-foot dance club featuring a top-40 format with a sprinkling of country hits. **City Rock** offers live music every night. Whatever you're looking for, you'll probably find it at OKC's Citywalk. (*$–$$, (405) 232-WALK, citywalkokc.com*) ❸ **Kongo's:** If you're in the mood to groove, you can dance the night away at this 10,000-square-foot facility. Kongo's has a (very) large dance floor, a cigar lounge, some private lounges, and daily specials that are always running. They feature a nice mix of DJs and live bands, giving you yet more entertainment choices. If you want to shake your moneymaker, this is the place to do it. (*$–$$, (405) 579-5664*) ❹ **The Sooner Theatre:** Built in 1929 this Spanish Gothic–style theater is listed on the National Register of Historic Places. Both regional and national musicians, singers, actors, and other entertainers have stood in its spotlight, and many OU Fine Arts College performances take place here as well. It's one of the best places in town to hear a live band perform. (*$–$$$, (405) 321-9600, soonertheatre.com*)

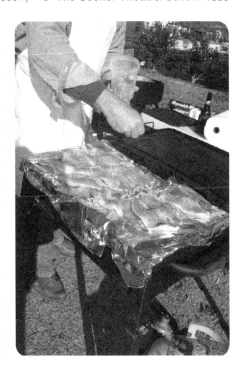

Shopping

❶ **The Apothem:** Located in the Campus Corner district, the Apothem is ground zero for all your OU gear. You can get tailgating supplies, men's and women's clothing, things for the home, kids' stuff, and much more. (*(405) 447-2345, theapothem.com*) ❷ **Campus Corner:** This shopping district was developed in the early 1900s to cater specifically to students and faculty at OU. Today it's a happily thriving commercial district with 75 local and national stores, restaurants, and bars. (*oucampuscorner.com*) ❸ **Green Door Mercantile:** This is one of the more eclectic gift shops you'll find, with merchandise literally all over the map and the globe. You can pick up anything from African tribal masks to nautical-themed tote bags. If nothing else you can pass a couple of hours in here without even trying. (*(405) 321-5522, gdoor.com*) ❹ **Tribes Gallery:** This art gallery specializes in Native American artists and artisans, with paintings, pottery, jewelry, baskets, sculptures, and more. Items include art from both local artists and internationally known artists like Doc Tate Navaquaya and Mirac Creeping Bear. (*(405) 329-4442*)

OKLAHOMA STATE

Oklahoma State University: 21,000 students
Stillwater, OK: pop. 39,065
Boone Pickens Stadium: seats 48,000
Colors: Orange and Black
Nickname: Cowboys
Mascot: Pistol Pete
Phone: (405) 744-5000

Visiting RVs park for free in Lot 81 on Hall of Fame Ave., east of the Physical Plant. Lot opens at 10:30 a.m. Tailgating runs from 10:30 a.m. until midnight including during game. No overnight parking. Leave pets at home; take garbage with you. Note: Childcare available at Stillwater YMCA for kids 3 and up, starting 1 hour before game and ending 1 hour after game's end.

Shuttle Info: Shuttle service provided to POSSE (season ticket holder/donor) parking lots.

Cowboys Media Partner: 93.7-FM KSPI

In 1890 the Oklahoma Territorial Legislature voted to create two universities as part of its efforts to create a more formal education system in the territory, which wouldn't become a state for another 17 years. One of those schools was in Norman; the other was in Stillwater.

The Oklahoma Territorial Agricultural and Mechanical College opened in December 1891—well, at least classes started. They met in local churches for nearly 3 years until the first college building opened, what became known as Old Central. The school dropped "Territorial" from its name when Oklahoma became a state in 1907, becoming Oklahoma A&M. (The school swapped that name for Oklahoma State University in 1957.)

Proud and immortal
Bright shines your name
Oklahoma State
We herald your fame
Ever you'll find us
Loyal and true
To our Alma Mater
O-S-U!

The university experienced its first major growth during the 22-year tenure of university president Henry Bennett, who developed a strategic plan for the campus and curriculum that was followed by administrators after him for the next half-century. OSU is executing its new campus master plan now, which is based on Bennett's.

I doubt Bennett anticipated the school's growth into the 21st century to have the reach it does, with satellite campuses spread across the state and a combined enrollment of almost 33,000, but OSU has earned a national reputation and made the Princeton Review's list as one of America's "Best Value" colleges.

OSU has not, historically, been one of America's best football programs. However it has produced some of the country's best running backs, earning the nickname "Tailback U."

It all began in 1901 when the territorial university played its first game. OSU didn't have a coach for the first four seasons, and it showed. The teams were a combined 3-13-4.

The Cowboys did have some successful seasons in the 1930s and 1940s, but OSU's best success came in the 1980s under Coach Pat Jones.

Jones coached the Cowboys for 11 seasons, including the school's only 10-win seasons in 1984, 1987, and 1988. He was helped by a couple of tailbacks named Thurman Thomas and Barry Sanders. During his 1988 junior year, Sanders led the nation with a record-setting 2,850 yards rushing and 44 touchdowns (including the Cowboys' bowl game) on his way to winning the Heisman Trophy.

But things went downhill quickly for Jones's Cowboys. In 1989, with Sanders off to the NFL, OSU went 4-7 in the first of eight straight losing seasons, including a winless campaign in 1991.

In 2005 OSU brought in a man to do as head coach what he did for the Cowboys as a player: win. Mike Grundy was the quarterback of those back-to-back 10-win seasons in the late 1980s and is still the game, season, and career passing leader in OSU history.

School Mascot

Like many A&M schools around the country, Oklahoma A&M teams were commonly called names like the Agriculturists, Farmers, and Aggies. The official nickname for the school was Tigers, but no one really liked that name.

Not the least of those disapproving of the school's monikers was a man named Charles Saulsberry who was a sports writer for the *Oklahoma City Times*. In 1924 he and several of his colleagues began calling the teams the A&M Cowboys—in his mind a much more fitting nickname. Most everyone else agreed, and within a couple of years Cowboys had taken hold.

At about the same time a U.S. Deputy Marshall in the area, Frank B. "Pistol Pete" Eaton, led Stillwater's Armistice Day Parade. He dressed in the image of "a tough, proud, self-reliant cowboy," according to the school's account. If you imagine the Wild West lawmen in the movies with big hats, jeans tucked into their boots, and a badge pinned to their coat, you'll have an accurate image of "Pistol Pete" Eaton.

A cartoon drawing of Eaton quickly became the school mascot, and Pistol Pete, the mascot, was a huge hit. Although that was in 1923, it wouldn't be until 1984 that the caricature and mascot name became official.

The costumed Pistol Pete you'll see walking the sidelines first appeared in 1958. Every year about a dozen students compete for the job of wearing the outfit, which consists of traditional cowboy attire and a really big headpiece that resembles "Pistol Pete" Eaton wearing his hat. ("Resembles" is the key word; in pictures his head wasn't really *that* big.)

Oklahoma State Fight Song

Cowboys a riding,
Lassoes a-flying,
Under the western sky.
And as they ride,
We rise to sing and shout our battle cry!
Ride, ride, ride, ride,
Ride 'em Cowboys,
Right down the field;
Fight! Fight! Fight! Fight!
Fight 'em Cowboys, and never yield.
Ride, ride, ride, ride,
Ride on, Cowboys, to victory;
Cross (opponent)'s goal;
Then we'll sing "O-kla-homa State!"

Game-Day Traditions
Spirit Rider and Bullet

In 1984 the OSU band director and the president of the OSU Rodeo Association got together and decided it would be a good idea to have a cowboy riding a horse to help enthuse fans and celebrate when the Cowboys scored. That's how the Spirit Rider tradition was born.

John Beall, the Rodeo Association president, used his own horse, Della, to ride along the field and celebrate Cowboys touchdowns. Students and fans loved the Spirit Rider, and in 1988 the university bought its own black horse to take over the duties. A student contest named the horse Bullet, and now Bullet and the Spirit Rider ride with the marching band at the beginning of the game and after each touchdown.

The Walk

It's a 21st-century tradition, but a popular one on game day in Stillwater.

The night before home games, the football team stays in the Atherton Hotel and the Student Union. On game day, 2 hours and 15 minutes before kickoff, the team emerges and walks down Hester Street to the stadium flanked by cheering fans and followed by the marching band and OSU spirit squad.

Visiting Oklahoma State

Stillwater was the first settlement in the Unassigned Lands, as the area now known as Oklahoma was called when it was ceded to the United States. (It was the only area not settled by Native Americans.) Today it is pretty much a stereotypical college town that revolves around OSU, which is also the city's largest employer.

Where to Stay

❶ The Atherton Hotel at OSU: Part of OSU's campus, the Atherton has 81 guest rooms and suites, furnished luxuriously enough to pass for a boutique hotel. Among the standard amenities are upgraded bath toiletries and robes, a 27-inch TV with DVD player, a DVD library, and in-room high-speed Internet. Rates during football weekends are $150 and $160. You can imagine this is a popular place on game weekends, so be sure to call ahead for reservations. Note that no one person can reserve more than three rooms at a time. (*(405) 744-6835, athertonhotel.okstate.edu)* ❷ The Country Chateau Inn Bed & Breakfast: Four minutes from OSU and downtown Stillwater, Country Chateau offers three suites and a private guest cottage on 8 acres. The cottage has two bedrooms and a sleeper sofa, kitchen, bath, satellite TV, and a private deck with

hot tub. Both suites and cottage are thematically decorated, ranging from Mission style to a floral motif. Guests may use the swimming pool. Rates are $100–$185, with a minimum two-night stay on football weekends. (*(405) 377-1328, bbonline.com/ok/country chateau/rooms.html*)

❸ Dancing Deer Lodge: Hidden on 5 wooded acres, this B&B offers three suites and has a unique, Native American theme. The suites have stocked refrigerators,

microwaves, TV/VCRs, coffeemakers, and private entries. Other features include a double Jacuzzi, fireplace, or log bed frame, depending on the suite. Displayed throughout the lodge is a large collection of Native American artwork, including Kachina dolls and pottery. Rates run $89–$165, depending on the suite and day of the week. Football weekends require a two-night stay. (*(800) 675-5684, bbonline.com/ok/dancingdeer*) ❹ **Lake Carl Blackwell Campgrounds:** You'll find 185 RV sites spread over seven campgrounds (eight including the equestrian campground) here. Not all sites have utility hookups. If you want electric and water, reserve space at Turkey Hollow or Deer Run campgrounds. For electric only go to Pine Grove or Fox Run campgrounds. If you're cool with roughing it, Beaver Cove and HPELS offer plenty of space. Sites with both electric and water go quickly, so call as far in advance as you can. Rates run anywhere from $8 (no hookups) to $22 (water and electric). The park also offers some cabins. (*(405) 744-3855, vpaf.okstate.edu/LCB/Campgrounds.htm*)

Where to Eat

TAILGATER SUPPLIES: ❶ **Asian Food Mart:** This small, but well-organized store is about the only place in town to get exotic groceries. The good news is they have a pretty decent selection of spices, frozen foods, and offbeat items. (*(405) 624-6668*) ❷ **Stillwater Farmers' Market:** This market offers seasonal, locally grown produce, breads, jellies, sausages, enchiladas, salsa, and other foods. During warmer weather, the market is outside in Stillwater's Strickland Park, from 8 a.m. until 1 p.m., Saturday and Wednesday. From November to March, the market is located on West 9th St., inside the NewsPress Lobby, every Saturday from 9 a.m. to 12 noon. (*(405) 624-1251, stillwaterfarmersmarket.com*)

SPORTS BARS: ❸ **Eskimo Joe's:** They placed third in *Sports Illustrated*'s "Perfect 10 College Sports Bars." Maybe it's the cold beer; maybe it's the top-quality pub grub. Or it could be the stupendous Joe Dome: a retractable, curved glass roof that slides open or closed, depending on the weather. Inside, you'll find a cheerful two-story saloon, decorated with old signs and ads. In between these are 15 TVs, including a projection and a widescreen plasma TV—and a whole lot of people having fun. (*$, (800) 256-JOES, eskimojoes.com*)

RESTAURANTS: ❹ **Bad Brad's Barbecue:** One of four, Stillwater's was the second Bad Brad's to open. Inside this red-trimmed stone house, you'll find a

rustic-style dining room, protected by a large stuffed bear. Brad's gets kudos from local residents for their slow-cooked meats—like 13 hours of slow smoking over a wood fire (gas and electric cooking are strictly verboten). The results are deeply flavored, meltingly tender brisket, ribs, and other offerings, like sausage, chicken, and turkey. (*$, (405) 377-4141, badbrads.com*) ❺ Mexico Joe's: This attractively designed cantina has a menu of Sonoran-style Mexican food, with a few American dishes tossed in. This translates to fajitas, tamales, enchiladas, and other familiar Mexican classics. If you're thinking this restaurant's name sounds awfully familiar, you're right. Mexico Joe's is owned by the same guys as Eskimo Joe's. It's also a big OSU alumni hangout. (*$, (405) 372-1169, mexicojoes.com*) ❻ The Rancher's Club: Relatively new to Stillwater, and part of OSU's Atherton Hotel, this upscale restaurant offers an atmosphere of rich hardwoods, soft leather seating, eye-catching paintings, and bronze sculpture. If you want the best steak in town, this is where to go. Unlike many steakhouses the entrée comes with a couple of sides. (*$$, (405) 744-BEEF, theranchersclub.com*) ❼ Shortcakes Diner: Whether you want your breakfast at 12 midnight or 12 noon, they've got you covered. Shortcakes is an important first stop for many OSU fans on game days to get properly fueled for a day of tailgating. The coffee is strong, the hash browns are addictive, and the omelets are a local legend. And the atmosphere? It's classic diner cozy. (*$, (405) 624-1057*)

Daytime Fun

❶ **National Wrestling Hall of Fame & Museum:** This off-beat, but serious museum honors amateur and Olympic wrestling champions—no WWF here. Inside you'll see the Museum of Wrestling History, FILA International Hall of Fame, Wall of Champions, and Hall of Founders. The museum displays sculptures, photographs, banners, plaques, medals, trophies, uniforms, and other memorabilia. There are some fun and educational interactive displays, too. Admission is free, but there's a suggested donation of $5 per adult, $2 per child, $10 per family, and $25 for group tours. (*Free, (405) 377-5243, wrestlinghalloffame.org*) ❷ **OSU Botanical Garden:** It might be hot, flat, and dusty everywhere else in town, but this Botanical Garden is like a cool, green oasis. The Garden covers approximately 100 acres, including the Oklahoma Gardening Studio Grounds. Inside the Grounds are 3 acres of display gardens

containing more than 300 plant varieties. You can walk in and enjoy this little corner of Eden anytime except Wednesdays; that's when they tape *Oklahoma Gardening*. If you'd like a guided tour, you'll need to make an appointment. (*Free, (405) 744-5404, hortla.okstate.edu*) ❸ **Woodland Park Vineyard:** While some wineries and vineyards can claim a long history of winegrowing, the owners of this vineyard only began picking grapes in August of 2004. Their beautifully landscaped vineyard is open for tastings Thursday through Saturday. Winery tours are available on Saturdays and by appointment. The tasting room features wines made on-site, and lots of wine accessories available for purchase. Homemade jellies and breads and local artwork are also for sale. (*$, (405) 743-2442, woodlandparkvineyards.com*)

Nighttime Fun

❶ **Roosters:** Here you'll walk into a lively college hotspot. The drink selection is strong here, and the prices are college-student cheap, which is even better. There's almost always a crowd, and it can get loud—but isn't that what you want in a college bar? (*$, (405) 372-9278*) ❷ **Tumbleweed Dance Halls and**

Concert Arena: The Tumbleweed is a venue for top recording country stars, as well as rock and alternative groups such as Vanilla Ice, Eve Six, Jackyl, and Third Eye Blind. What started as a dance hall and restaurant now spans across 65 acres and has outdoor rodeo and concert arenas. The rodeo arena seats 3,000, while the concert arena holds 8,000, with reserve and general admission seats available for most shows. Both are capped with an 85-foot flagpole flying the largest American flag in this region. When the flag's flying, you know an outdoor event's happening. (*$–$$$, (405) 377-0075, www.calffry.com*) ❸ **Willie's Saloon:** Located on the strip in Stillwater, Willie's has been a tradition almost since it opened its doors in 1974. It was the site of Garth Brooks's first public performance and still showcases some of the best new up-and-coming country talent. If you're in the mood for a cold drink and some hot country music, Willie's is a safe bet. (*$, (405) 377-7716*)

Shopping

Campus Corner: Just across the street from the OSU Campus, you'll find a small collection of university and student oriented shops. If you're looking for

OSU gear, you should stop into **Chris's University Spirit**. These guys have a huge inventory of Cowboy wear for everybody in the family. They also have some more unique items since most of their clothing is decorated in-house by their own graphic artists. (*(800) 222-6670, chrisuniversityspirit.com*) If you need regular clothes (at least, if you're a woman) stop into **Elizabeth's** or the **Wooden Nickel**. Both stock some very nice wares, with the Nickel leaning toward younger, more trendy styles. (*Elizabeth's (405) 377-3424; The Wooden Nickel (405) 377-8808*) If all that shopping leaves you hungry, there're places to grab a bite, like **Hideaway Pizza**, Stillwater's original pizza shop.

TEXAS

University of Texas: 36,878 students
Austin, TX: pop. 690,252
Royal-Memorial Stadium: seats 80,082
Colors: Burnt Orange and White
Nickname: Longhorns
Mascot: Bevo
Phone: (512) 478-1833

Non-Longhorn Foundation RV parking available in Lot 115 on a space-available basis. Check-in begins at 3 p.m. Thursday before home games. Fee is $350 per game. Cars park for $5 to $10 depending on lot. Tailgating runs 5 p.m. Friday, until 2 hours after game's end. No open flames allowed in parking garages. Be mindful of local open container laws.

Shuttle Info: Capital Metro provides shuttle service, $5 round trip. Pick-up locations are UT Intramural Fields parking lots at 51st and Guadalupe St., and northwest side of Barton Creek Mall.

Longhorns Media Partner: 98.1 KVET

Efforts to build a university in what is now Austin began as far back as 1827 when aspirations were included in the constitution for the Mexican state of Coahuila y Texas. It never happened.

In 1836 Texas gained independence from Mexico, and the new country included in its constitution plans building a university and set aside land near the capitol building as College Hill. It never happened.

In 1846 Texas became a state, and the legislature appropriated money to finally start building the school. It never happened. This time succession and the Civil War got in the way.

Later the Morrill Act of 1862 provided land for state universities. In Texas, Texas A&M was that university.

Finally, in 1876, the Texas Constitution called for "a university of the first class," and this time it happened. In September of 1883 the University of Texas welcomed its first students on College Hill.

Constitutional restrictions on building made early growth difficult for the university, but a combination of land sales, endowments, and revenue from oil sales allowed UT to grow into one of the largest universities in the country with nearly 50,000 total students (including graduate students), ranking it the fifth largest in the United States. It is ranked as one of the nation's "Public Ivy" schools (state schools considered to have the educational credentials of Ivy League schools) and has one of the top-ranked business schools in America.

It also has one of the top-ranked football programs in America.

The Longhorns have the third best overall record in college football history. Only Notre Dame and Michigan have won more games. Among those wins are four national championships (1963, 1969, 1970, and 2005). Two Texas running backs have won the coveted Heisman Trophy: Earl Campbell (1977) and Ricky Williams (1998).

All of this success began in 1893 when Texas played its first four games and ran the table. There was a lot more success to follow. In fact, only one UT coach in history left the job with a sub-.500 winning percentage—Jack Chevigny's .483 for his three seasons in the 1930s.

But the Longhorns truly became a national power when Darrell Royal took over in 1957.

For UT, 1956 was a miserable year—the worst ever. They went 1-9. No one expected too much more of them the next season. But Coach Royal did. The 1957 Longhorns went 6-4-1 and earned a trip to the Sugar Bowl. Royal never had a losing season in his 20 years at Texas. His teams won 11 conference championships, went to 16 bowl games, and won 3 national championships. He retired with a 167-47-5 record, still far-and-away the most wins of any Texas coach. That's one reason why the Longhorns now play in Darrell K. Royal–Texas Memorial Stadium.

The 'Horns had some rough years in the late 1980s and 1990s, but things turned back around in 1998 when Mack Brown took over the program, inherited a 5-6 team, and turned it into a 9-3 team the next season. He's continued to win, including the national championship in 2005.

School Mascot

While Bevo might be the best-known mascot in the country, he wasn't Texas's first. That honor goes to Pig, a pit bull dog. The longhorn didn't show up until halftime of the 1916 Texas–Texas A&M game. A couple of cowboys pulled a frightened

"Texas, Fight"

Texas, Fight! Texas, Fight! and it's
goodbye to A&M.
Texas, Fight! Texas, Fight!
and we'll put over one more win.
Texas, Fight! Texas, Fight!
for it's Texas we love best!
Give 'em hell! Give 'em hell! Go, Horns,
Go! and it's goodbye to all the rest.

(Chanted)
Yeah, orange!
Yeah, white!
Yeah, Longhorns, fight, fight, FIGHT!
Texas, FIGHT!
Texas, FIGHT!
Yeah, Texas, FIGHT!
Texas, FIGHT!
Texas, FIGHT!
Yeah, Texas, FIGHT!

longhorn steer onto the field where a group of Texas alumni presented it as the new mascot. The animal's name was Bo.

The editor of the *Texas Exes Alcalae* magazine, in his rushed-to-press story celebrating the new, live mascot, wrote, "His name is Bevo. Long may he reign!" There are several theories why he picked that name, but no one is sure.

The most likely, perhaps, is that there was a series of comic strips at the time that featured monkeys as main characters who were named for their character's traits—the detective was Sherlocko, for example. They were very popular comics, and legend has it that's where the Marx Brothers got their names: Groucho, Harpo, and Chico. Maybe that's the way the Longhorn got the name Bevo. Maybe not.

The story that isn't true is the one of legend. It's the one about how a group of rival Texas A&M pranksters branded the score of a game the Aggies won on the Texas mascot. The score was 13–0. UT students, to avoid prolonged embarrassment, converted the 13 into a B, the dash into an e, stuck in a v, and with the 0 it spelled Bevo.

In 1917 some A&M students did in fact brand the steer with the famous 13–0 score (which was from the 1915 game), but it had nothing to do with naming it Bevo.

Game-Day Traditions
Big Bertha

The Longhorn Band claims Big Bertha is the largest drum in the world. (There are a couple of other drums that claim that, too, however.) It's 8 feet in diameter, more than 3 1/2 feet deep, and stands 10 feet tall on its cart. The band wheels the 500-pound instrument—dubbed the Sweetheart of the Longhorn Band—onto the field for its halftime show and for other performances.

The drum also has what has to be one of the most interesting histories of any instrument anywhere.

It was commissioned in 1922 by the University of Chicago to foster team spirit. But when Chicago shuttered its football program it discarded the drum—sticking it under the stadium. It sat there for decades and was contaminated by atomic bomb research conducted at the stadium in the 1940s.

In 1955 Col. D. Harold Byrd decided that Texas should have the largest drum in the world (he was a former band member and proud of his alma mater) so he bought the drum from the University of Chicago. The price: $1.

After he had it decontaminated and restored, Byrd donated Big Bertha to the Longhorn Band.

"The Eyes of Texas"

The Eyes of Texas are upon you all
the live long day.

The Eyes of Texas are upon you, you
cannot get away.

Do not think you can escape them at
night or early in the morn.

The Eyes of Texas are upon you 'till
Gabriel blows his horn.

Hook 'em Horns

Hand symbols have a long history among Texas universities—especially those in the old Southwest Conference—but the best known around the country is Texas's Hook 'em Horns.

It was introduced at a pep rally in 1955 and quickly became the primary school symbol among students. The hand sign is made by extending your index and pinky fingers while holding your two middle fingers with your thumb. It resembles the Longhorn logo on the football team's helmets, which is also the university's logo. Today it's almost as recognizable as that logo, too. *Sports Illustrated* even featured it on the cover of an issue in 1973.

The Tower

When the Main Tower Building was constructed in the 1930s, the man overseeing the project, Carl Eckhardt, Jr., decided it needed a lighting system to celebrate university achievements. So he had added to the architecture a system of lights that can bathe the 27-story tower in several patterns of orange and white. The first orange lighting was in 1937. Over time Eckhardt realized there needed to be a system to the popular tradition, so he created one.

Eckhardt's system was pretty basic: a number 1 on all sides highlighted with orange lights meant Texas won a national championship. It lit up all orange to celebrate a victory over Texas A&M or Commencement or other significant accomplishments as decided by the university president, and an orange top signified other athletic victories.

In 2001 the school created new, much more detailed criteria for lighting patterns, but it still glows all orange for football victories.

Visiting Texas

The first Anglo colonists—led by Texas's founding father Stephen F. Austin—settled in these buffalo hunting grounds in 1822. But it wasn't until Texas president Mirabeau B. Lamar (Texas was a country then) decided to move the seat of government from Houston to the settlement then known as Waterloo in 1838 that things really took off. The population of Austin has doubled every 20 years since its establishment (it's now the 16th largest city in the country) and is consistently found on "Best City" lists. Austin is known as the Live Music Capital of the World and is also home to Dell Computers (not that the two are related).

Where to Stay

❶ Austin Folk House Bed and Breakfast: Consistently atop "Best of Austin" lists, this B&B offers all the amenities and services you would expect a top-notch place to provide. It also offers one you wouldn't expect: a cocker spaniel. You can add the house dog to your room for $20 if you miss having someone paw you at night. Rooms run $85–$225 (without the dog). (*(866) 472-6700, austinfolkhouse.com*) ❷ Austin Lone Star RV Resort: About a 5-minute drive south of downtown, this park has

spacious pull-throughs with full hookups. You can get phone hookups on premium sites, and wireless Internet is available for an added fee. The park also has an on-site lodge with a full-service restaurant, heated swimming pool, and enclosed hot tub. If you need some last minute tailgate items, there's a convenience store on-site. Rates run $26–$47. (*(512) 444-6322, austinlonestar.com*) ❸ **The Driskill:** A cattle baron built this property in 1886 to be his showplace. It's still a showplace. They renovated the place in 1999 but kept the look and feel the original owner created, including a stained-glass dome ceiling in the lobby. The renovation updated all of the rooms, including Internet access. There are two on-site restaurants run by chef David Bull who, if you're a fan of The Food Network's *Iron Chef America*, you saw battling Bobby Flay on an episode. Rooms run $205–$300. (*(800) 252-9367, driskillhotel.com*) ❹ **Inn at Pearl Street:** Here you can stay in rooms in the main house or in a separate cottage on the walled property. If you want to add a little romance or luxury to your stay, there are several pampering packages available. Be sure to request a room with a Jacuzzi or private balcony. Rooms run $89–$200. (*(800) 494-2261, innpearl.com*) ❺ **La Hacienda RV Park and Resort:** La Hacienda has 53 sites with the basic amenities, including wireless Internet service. It also has some added features, such as a concierge service, a business center, and shower facilities built to ADA standards. You can rent cabins here, too. Sites cost $39–$47. (*(888) 378-7275, campingfriend.com /LaHaciendaRVPark*) ❻ **The Mansion at Judges Hill:** You can walk to campus from this Victorian-era mansion that was originally presented as a wedding gift by Thomas Dudley Wooten, one of the founders of the University of Texas. The mansion has been very well maintained, and some of its rooms are stunning reminders of how homes used to be built. Loaded with amenities, there is also a restaurant and lounge on-site. Rooms will set you back $99–$299. (*(800) 311-1619, mansionatjudgeshill.com*)

Where to Eat

TAILGATER SUPPLIES: ❶ **Central Market:** If you want someone else to do your tailgate cooking, you can pick up complete meals here. But for the rest of us, both locations are good choices to get fresh produce, meats, seafood, flowers, and specialty food items. There's also a full-service deli, baked goods, and imports from all over the world. (*N. Lamar Blvd. (512) 206-1000, Westgate (512) 899-4300, centralmarket.com*)

SPORTS BARS: ❷ **Cain and Abel's:** Come by on game day, and you'll see why many consider this the place to be on game day. There are more than a dozen TVs, plus pool and foosball tables for when you're finished watching the game. You can hang out and order from the typical sports bar menu on an upstairs deck and a downstairs patio. (*$, (512) 476-3201, cainandabels.com*) ❸ **The Tavern:** Built with European plans to resemble a German public house, The Tavern has been an Austin favorite since 1916. You'll find TVs scattered all around the place and pool tables and video games upstairs. This tavern also serves breakfast—but you do have to go home between last call and breakfast. (*$, (512) 320-8377, austintavern.com*) ❹ **Texas Showdown Saloon:** This place has the feel a real Texas saloon should. Close to campus, it has lots of atmosphere (although not a lot of TVs), a beer garden outside, and pool tables inside. Your football game-day bonus: free hotdogs. (*$, (512) 472-2010, showdowns oftexas.com/austin/games.cfm*)

RESTAURANTS: ❺ **Dan McKlusky's Sixth Street:** This is Texas, and this is a good place to get a big steak. People have been doing that since 1979. In addition to the aged steaks, the menu offers seafood and a variety of side dishes. There's a valet out front—let him park your car. Parking can be tricky downtown. (*$$$, (512) 473-8924,* *danmckluskys.com*) ❻ **Earl Campbell's BBQ Restaurant & Bar:** He lit up the scoreboard when he played at UT—winning the Heisman Trophy in 1977—and now he helps light up Sixth Street with his restaurant and bar. You'll find the memorabilia you expect here (yes, including that famous trophy), but you'll also find good food served in large portions. Although the name says barbecue, the menu has other things, too. (*$, (512) 397-3275*) ❼ **Fino Restaurant Patio & Bar:** Asti is one of Austin's favorite places to eat, and the folks who own it have followed up that hit with Fino, a casual Spanish place that features an open dining room and a room with tall bistro tables. Tapas rule here, of course. A local favorite is the creamy fried goat cheese with onion jam and honey. (*$, (512) 474-2905, astiaustin.com*) ❽ **Las Palmas:** You'll find real, traditional Mexican food at this "Best of Austin" eatery. Northern Mexican cuisine is the specialty here. Try any of the enchiladas. If you're driving along East Seventh Street looking for the place, keep an eye out for the building with all the Christmas lights strung around the outside of the building. (*$, (512) 457-4944*)

Daytime Fun

❶ **Austin Duck:** This is the most unique tour of Austin you'll take. The Austin Duck is an amphibious vehicle that drives around downtown so you can see the capitol,

governor's mansion, historic Congress Avenue, and other sites. Then it drives into Lake Austin. Really. This land and water tour of the city is popular, so be sure to make reservations. (*$$, (512) 477-5274, austinducks.com*)

❷ **Austin Zoo:** While the Austin Zoo looks a lot like other zoos, it isn't. This zoo is a "rescue zoo"—more than 90 percent of the animals have been rescued from circuses, improper residences, and research laboratories. (*$, (512) 288-1490, austinzoo.org*)

❸ **Congress Avenue Bridge:** This is the Bat Bridge. The famous crime-fighter doesn't emerge from the bridge. Real bats do—1.5

million of them, every evening from March to November. The bats are Mexican free-tailed bats that have lived under the bridge for years. When it was refurbished in 1980, so many bats came to roost that it is now the largest urban bat colony in North America. You can view their massive flight from several spots nearby or from a bat-watching boat cruise on Town Lake. One tip: take an umbrella when you go (and it's not for the rain). (Free, Downtown)   ❹ **Lyndon Baines Johnson Library and Museum:** The LBJ Library is home to 40 million pages of history, detailing the entire public career of the 36th president of the United States. The museum also has permanent historical and cultural exhibits, as well as changing exhibitions and special activities. (*Free, (512) 721-0200, lbjlib.utexas.edu*) ❺ **State Capitol:** The Texas State Capitol Building, built in 1888, is the largest in gross square footage of all state capitols, and is taller than the U.S. Capitol Building (by 15 feet). The Renaissance Revival–style building is made of Texas pink granite and native limestone and was designated a National Historic Landmark in 1986. There are about 22 acres of surrounding grounds and 17 historic monuments. (*Free, (512) 475-3070, tspb.state.tx.us/SPB/Capitol/TexCap.htm*) ➏ **Wonder World:** This is America's only earthquake-formed cave, and it's the state's most visited. But your trip includes more than just a cave. Ride the elevator to the peak of the 110-foot Tejas Observation Tower, and enjoy the view of the Texas Hill Country. Or take a train ride through the waterfalls of Mystery Mountain into the wildlife petting park, or play in the Anti-Gravity House. There are also picnic areas. (*$$, (877) 492-4657, wonderworldpark.com*)

Nighttime Fun

➊ **Antone's:** Antone's is arguably Austin's most famous music venue (but there are several good ones in town). The stage here hosts some famous names playing the blues and funk, as well as a stable of local artists. Live blues seven nights a week. (*$–$$, (512) 474-5315, antones.net*)   ➋ **Elephant Room:** Drawing a hip, upscale crowd for live music every night of the year, the Elephant Room is always atop Austin's "Best of" lists for jazz bars. The club features local and national acts. (*$, (512) 473-2279, natespace.com/elephant*) ➌ **Oslo:** Oslo is "a bastion of cool sophistication and Nordic serenity." That's not me saying that, that's from *Condé Nast Traveler*. Long and

narrow, with minimalist retro '60s decor, this bar offers hip drinks and a diverse menu—including fondue. If you want to get away from the typical college crowd, this is a good place to do it. Wednesday is all-day happy hour. (*$, (512) 480-9433, osloaustin.com*) ❹ **Sixth Street and the Warehouse Entertainment District:** This is really the only place you need to go. Throughout the district there are scores of restaurants and live music nightspots, including some of Austin's best live music venues like Emo's, Stubb's, and the Red-Eyed Fly. You'll have a great night just hopping in and out of the clubs here.

Shopping

❶ **26 Doors:** Located in the Midtown shopping district, this collection of quaint boutique stores is a cozy little shopping center with a variety of interesting shops and restaurants. (*(512) 451-8331*) ❷ **The Drag:** Technically it's Guadalupe Street, but everyone calls it The Drag. Bordering UT, the area is home to many of Austin's coolest shops including music stores, vintage clothing, and a variety of locally owned shops and restaurants. The outdoor Renaissance Market here has jewelry, clothing, and gifts made by Austin artisans. ❸ **SoCo:** SoCo stands for South Congress Avenue, and it's the hottest, hippest area in town. This old warehouse district has been revitalized and is now home to artisans, funky antiques, vintage clothing shops, interesting boutiques, restaurants, clubs, and more. ❹ **University Co-op:** This nonprofit has been outfitting Longhorn fans since 1896 with anything they need (and a whole lot they don't need but want) that is orange and white and has a Longhorn on it. From Spring Break essentials and guitar picks, to game-day attire and tailgate gear, you'll find it here. (*(800) 255-1896, universitycoop.com*)

TEXAS A&M

Texas A&M University: 45,083 students
College Station, TX: pop. 82,429
Kyle Field: seats 82,600
Colors: Maroon and White
Nickname: Aggies
Mascot: Reveille
Phone: (979) 862-2551

Visiting RVs park in Lot 100E, at $60 for the weekend, by online reservation only. Visitors can arrive early as 3 p.m. Friday, stay until 2 p.m. Sunday. Tailgating starts 5 hours prior to kickoff, continues through game until 2 p.m. Sunday. Post Oak Mall has free parking with shuttle service. No tailgating in parking garages. No parking in grass or lawns; no parking in streets or bike lanes.

Shuttle Info: Free shuttle from Post Oak Mall lots runs 3 hours prior to kickoff, until 2 hours after game.

Aggies Media Partner: 1620-AM WTAW

The Agricultural and Mechanical College of Texas was the first public institution of higher learning in Texas. Established in 1871 as a land-grant college, its mission was, primarily, to teach agriculture and mechanical arts, as well as military tactics. When it opened its doors in 1876, the college was an all-male military college. All students were required to be members of the Corps of Cadets (a requirement that wasn't dropped until 1965).

The Corps has always been a central part of life at Texas A&M and an important part of America's military history. Members of the Corps have served in every American conflict since the Spanish-American War. During World War II TAMU (as the school is often referred to) produced more than

20,000 Aggies who served in combat. Of those more than 14,000 served as officers; that's more officers than served from the U.S. Military and Naval Academies combined.

Today the Corps is one of only six federal, senior military colleges with active members and includes two Air Force Wings, two Army Brigades, and two Navy and Marine Regiments. It also includes the Fightin' Texas Aggie Band, which is a precision military marching band and the largest military marching band in the country.

While still a central part of campus life and the school's history, several other disciplines and curriculums have developed at the school. The name was changed to Texas A&M in 1963 to reflect that. Incidentally, officially the A&M have no meaning and are just a tie to the university's past.

A&M is one of just a handful of schools that are land-, sea-, and space-grant colleges, has one of the nation's top-ranked veterinary schools, and is home to the George Bush Presidential Library (that would be Bush 41).

It is also home to a football program that at times has been both horrible and great. It has some of the richest traditions of any program in the country (due in part to the Corps of Cadets) and has more people turn out for its Midnight Yell pep rally than some schools have show up to watch their games. More on that later, though.

Football got its start in College Station in 1894. The team played two games and split them—beating Galveston High School and losing to the University of Texas. The next year TAMU didn't field a team.

Football returned in 1896, and the team had mostly good years through the first half of the 20th century, highlighted by an 11-0 run in 1939, outscoring regular season opponents 198–18, and winning the national championship.

But as the second half of the 20th century opened, the team's fortunes fell. From 1948 to 1972 there was just one A&M coach whose tenure ended with a winning percentage above .500. That was Paul "Bear" Bryant's .634.

Bryant coached at A&M before moving on to legendary status at Alabama. In 1954 he inherited a team he felt was poor, weak, and untrained. He held a 10-day summer football camp in nearby Junction, Texas, to fix that. While today the camp would be considered unsafe, at the time it was a way to toughen up a team. The intense workouts began before dawn and ended with meetings just before midnight. At the time Texas was suffering from drought and a heat wave—the high temperature was never below 100°F. No water breaks were allowed, and for relief there were just two towels soaked in water—one for the offense and one for the

"Aggie War Hymn"

(Traditionally the first verse is omitted)

Hullabaloo, Caneck! Caneck!
Hullabaloo, Caneck! Caneck!

(First Verse)

All hail to dear old Texas A&M,
Rally around Maroon and White,
Good luck to the dear old Texas Aggies,
They are the boys who show the real old fight.
That good old Aggie spirit thrills us.
And makes us yell and yell and yell;
So let's fight for dear old Texas A&M,
We're goin' to beat you all to
Chig-gar-roo-gar-rem!
Chig-gar-roo-gar-rem!
Rough! Tough!
Real stuff! Texas A&M!

(Second Verse)

Good-bye to Texas University.
So long to the Orange and White.
Good luck to the dear old Texas Aggies,
They are the boys who show
*   the real old fight.*
"The eyes of Texas are upon you."
That is the song they sing so well . . .
Sounds like hell.
So, good-bye to Texas University,
We're goin' to beat you all to
Chig-gar-roo-gar-rem!
Chig-gar-roo-gar-rem!
Rough! Tough!
Real stuff! Texas A&M!

defense to share. Not many made it through the camp; the numbers vary, but somewhere around 30 of about 100 who signed up for the team were still standing after camp. Those survivors are known as the Junction Boys, and their story is in a book by Jim Dent, which became an ESPN movie.

All of that may have toughened up the team, but it didn't win games. That year the team went 1-9. But the next three years, Bryant's teams ended the season ranked second, first, and third in the Southwest Conference.

John David Crow wasn't one of the Junction Boys, but he did play for "Bear" Bryant. And he did well. Very well, winning the Heisman Trophy in 1957.

Some of the best Aggie teams played in the 1980s and 1990s under coaches Jackie Sherrill and R. C. Slocum. Their squads often won the conference and appeared in 14 bowl games in 21 seasons.

School Mascot

Like many agricultural and mechanical colleges founded about the same time, Texas A&M teams were called the Aggies. The difference is they never changed the name.

The Aggie teams are represented by Reveille—a purebred collie that became a mascot by accident. Literally.

The first Reveille wasn't purebred. She was a mutt that several members of the Fightin' Texas Aggie Band hit on their way home from a party in 1931. After the accident they picked up the dog and brought it home to take to the vet school the next day. But at dawn, when the Corps bugler played "Reveille," the dog began to bark. It had found a name and a home.

When football season began Reveille was named the official mascot and led the band onto the field. She wore a maroon-and-white jacket and roamed the sidelines during the game. Reveille was given the rank of Cadet General and when she died in 1944 was given a formal military funeral.

In recognition of the number of soldiers and officers A&M contributed to World War II, Reveille was given the honorary title of Cadet General by the U.S. Army and now all Reveilles hold that title.

Later the tradition of purebred collie Reveilles took hold, and the one you'll see on game day is Reveille VII. All previous Reveilles are buried side by side in a cemetery on the north side of Kyle Field.

Game-Day Traditions
The 12th Man

In 1922 TAMU was playing top-ranked Centre College, and it wasn't going well. The underdog Aggies were depleted by injuries as the game wore on, and the coach feared he might run out of players.

He remembered that a former player—who now played basketball at the school—was in the press box helping identify players, and he called for him. The student, E. King Gill, came down, suited up, and was ready to go in. He didn't need to (and the Aggies upset Centre College 22–14), but he became known as "The 12th Man," ready to go if the 11 players needed him.

That spirit captured the imagination of the student body, and before long the student body represented The 12th Man—standing the entire game to show their support. They still do.

In the late 1980s the tradition took another form when Coach Jackie Sherrill allowed regular students (who won the jobs during tryouts) to suit-up as The 12th Man kickoff team. They did well, but later Coach R. C. Slocum changed the new tradition to allow just one regular student to be on the kickoff team.

The 12th Man is also in song, sung by the student body after games A&M loses.

"The Twelfth Man"
Texas Aggies down in Aggieland,
We've got Aggie Spirit to a man.

"Stand united!" That's the Aggie theme,
We're the 12th Man on the team.
When we're down, the goin's rough and tough,
We just grin and yell: "We've got the stuff
To fight together for the Aggie dream."
We're the 12th Man on that FIGHTIN' AGGIE TEAM!

Gig 'Em

At the 1930 Yell Practice before the Aggies played the TCU Horned Frogs, Pinky Downs, an A&M graduate who sat on the Board of Regents at the time, shouted to the crowd, "What are we going to do to those Horned Frogs?" He answered his own question with, "Gig 'Em, Aggies!" while making a fist with his thumb extended. (A gig, by the way, is a spear-type tool used for hunting frogs.)

The hand symbol and phrase quickly caught on, and it is considered to have been the first hand symbol in the hand symbol–rich Southwest Conference.

"The Spirit of Aggieland"

Some may boast of prowess bold
Of the schools they think so grand,
But there's a spirit can ne'er be told
It's the Spirit of Aggieland.

Chorus:
We are the Aggies; the Aggies are we,
True to each other as Aggies can be,
We've got to FIGHT boys,
We've got to fight!
We've got to fight for Maroon and White.
After they've boosted all the rest,
They will come and join the best,
For we are the Aggies—the Aggies are we,
We're from Texas AMC
(Yell sequence that follows; traditionally
deleted at Muster)
T-E-X-A-S A-G-G-I-E,
Fight! Fight! Fight-fight-fight!
Fight! Maroon! White-White-White!
A-G-G-I-E
Texas! Texas! A-M-C!
Gig 'em, Aggies, 1-2-3
Farmers fight! Farmers fight!
Fight! Fight!
Farmers, farmers fight!
Fight! Fight! Fight! A! Whoop!

Midnight Yell Practice

It began as an after-dinner activity in the early 1900s when different Corps companies would gather "to learn heartily the old time pep," as the university puts it.

But in 1931 it took on a new look (and new meaning) when a group of cadets gathered in a room before the annual game against the University of Texas. Someone suggested all the freshman should fall out and meet on the steps of the YMCA building at midnight. The group told the senior yell leaders of the idea, and while they said it couldn't be sanctioned, maybe they'd show up.

They did show up, and when the freshmen began arriving, they found the YMCA building lit up with flares, and the first Midnight Yell Practice began.

In the years since, Yell Practice has grown. Today it's held in Kyle Field (thousands often show up) the night before the home game and at the Arches the Thursday night before an away game.

There's also a site dedicated at all away games for TAMU faithful to meet the night before the game.

Yell leaders, accompanied by the band, lead fans through old army yells, school cheers, and songs. They also tell fables of what the Aggies will do to their opponents. When Yell Practice is done, the lights go out, and all Aggies kiss their dates. (If they don't have a date, they have to "flick a Bic" to make it easier for two dateless people to find a kiss in the dark.)

Visiting Texas A&M

College Station owes its name to the fact that Texas A&M is here and is located along a railroad (originally the Houston and Texas Central Railway). Together with sister-city Bryan, the area is home to about 200,000 people. Pretty smart ones, too. At least according to *Money Magazine,* which in 2006 named College Station the most educated city in Texas and 11th in America. The size of the university is why it got that ranking. Its size is also why life in the area revolves

around TAMU, and College Station has the feel of a typical college town.

Where to Stay

❶ Marino Road RV Park: This new campground is a Passport America affiliate, so nightly rates can be half-price Sundays through Thursdays. But not during football weekends. It's in College Station's sister city, Bryan, but still pretty close to campus. The park has 76 sites with full hookups, cable TV, and wireless or modem Internet. Sites are graveled and level, with room to maneuver. Rates are $25 during A&M events, with a two-night stay required. Weekly rates are $120 with free cable. (*(979) 778-3767, marinoroadrv.com*) ❷ **Murphy's Bed & Breakfast:** A (very) short walk from campus, this one-story Victorian offers two guestrooms, each with a private bath. The rooms are furnished in a pared-down Victorian style—cleaner and simpler, more in keeping with a western climate. Guests get a full breakfast every day. Rooms run $100 and $125. (*(979) 696-7149, murphybed andbreakfast.com*) ❸ **The Villa at Messina Hof:** Part of the Messina Hof Winery and Resort, the Villa was once a convent. Today this luxurious B&B inn offers 10 guest rooms, each furnished in a different style—Victorian, Mediterranean, Art Deco, French, etc. All have private baths stocked with bathrobes. Rooms also feature wireless Internet and satellite TV. Stays include a winery tour, a wine and cheese reception, and a European-style full breakfast served with Champagne. Rooms will set you back $150–$299, with a two-night minimum stay during football weekends. (*(800) 736-9463, messinahof.com*)

❹ **Vineyard Court Designer Suites Hotel:** Located just two blocks from campus, suites are themed, with individualized furnishings that are definitely a cut above your average hotel chain. Nice touches include pillow-top mattresses, down comforters, and spacious kitchen areas. During A&M home games, studio and one-bedroom suites are $205, while two-bedroom and executive business suites are $255. A two-night minimum stay is required. (*(888) 846-2678, vineyardcourt.com*)

Where to Eat

TAILGATER SUPPLIES: ❶ **Brazos Valley Farmers' Market:** This small, friendly market is open Saturdays from 8 a.m. to 1 p.m. during autumn, at the corner of Texas Avenue and William J. Bryan Parkway. About 25 to 30 vendors sell locally grown produce, fruits, eggs, cheeses, jellies and jams, honey, herbs, and garden plants. (*(936) 870-4099, brazosvalleyfarmersmarket.com*)

SPORTS BARS: ❷ **The Corner:** Named "College Bar of the Month" by *Playboy*, the walls are dotted with huge flat-screen TVs so you can catch every minute of

the game. Patrons will even pull their trucks up to the back porch and down a pitcher or two. This rather new bar is well on its way to becoming a tradition—being only 20 yards from campus dorms with no cover charge and cheap drinks helps. The Corner hosts great pregame parties. (*$, (979) 268-1406, thecornerbcs.com*) ❸ **The Dixie Chicken:** This College Station legend is another *Playboy* fave and was named one of the "Top 20 Dive Bars in America" by *Stuff* magazine in 2002. The Chicken claims to serve more beer per square foot than any bar in the United States. Could be; it's certainly full of enough happy Aggies enjoying country music and cheap beer. Stay late and you can hear a Dixie Chicken tradition. Every night at closing time, they play "Goodnight Irene." The Dixie Chicken also could have gone in the Nighttime Fun section—it rocks whether it's game day or not. (*$, (979) 846-2322, dixiechicken.com*)

RESTAURANTS: ❹ **Christopher's World Grille:** Located in nearby Bryan, this beautifully restored 1913 ranch house is filled with carved Victorian mirrors and leopard-print rugs. Christopher's caters former President Bush's meals when he's in town, unless he decides to drop in. The menu changes seasonally, though steaks are always present. If you're not in the mood for steak, try the pastramied

Salmon or Tuscan veal loin. (*$$, (979) 776-2181, christophersworld grille.com*) ❺ **Mi Cocina:** This is where you want to have breakfast on game day. It's near A&M, and serves the best huevos rancheros and barbacoa (seasoned beef with eggs) you're likely to find. It's a great way to kick off your day, and maybe kill last night's hangover—excellent spicy comfort food, accompanied by murals, flashing lights, and a charmingly scruffy atmosphere. (*$, (979) 695-6666*)

❻ **Square One Bistro:** Square One was once a mortuary. Not that you could tell today—the dining room is hung with original art (part of a partnership between the Bistro and a local gallery) and filled with scarred wooden kitchen tables. The food is fresh, and has an Italian flair to it. Try the tomato-basil fondue on angel hair pasta, or the blackberry duck breast. Best of all, you'll be enjoying four-star food at regular-Joe prices. Located in Bryan. (*$, (979) 361-0264, squareonebryan.com*)

Daytime Fun

❶ **Brazos Valley Museum of Natural History:** This museum is full of fossils, sculptures, antique farming and survey equipment, and lots more stuff. There's also a discovery room with more than 15 varieties of live animals, dozens of stuffed animals, an active glass-front beehive, plus several revolving and temporary exhibits. If you only have time to see one or two things, definitely check out the Ice Age mammal exhibit and the dinosaur fossils (they have actual, fossilized dinosaur skin). Another cool feature—Game Day Learn & Play programs, held during every Aggie home football game. (*$, (979) 776-2195,*

bvmuseum.myriad.net) ❷ **Lake Bryan:** When the weather's hot—and it gets hot in Texas—you may want to take a swim in a lake. You're in luck. Lake Bryan has a sandy beach area where you can do just that. You can also play sand volleyball, go boating, fishing, camping, or biking, take a hike, or have a little picnic. Their mountain bike trail circles the lake for 16 strenuous miles. Camping is another option. (*$, (979) 361-0861, lakebryan.net*) ❸ **Monastery of St. Clare Miniature Horse Farm:** Yes, a monastery and a miniature horse farm, all in one. I don't make this stuff up. It's owned and operated by the Franciscan Poor Clare Nuns, who support themselves through the sale of their ceramics and other crafts, as well as the sale of their horses. There are self-guided and guided tours available to visitors Tuesday through Saturday 1:30 to 4 p.m. (Guided tours are given Monday through Friday, by reservation only.) (*$, (979) 836-9652, monasteryminiaturehorses.com/index.htm*)

Nighttime Fun

❶ **Fitzwilly's Live Music:** This down-home restaurant and bar has a menu full of home-cooked goodness ranging from burgers to chicken-fried chicken with cream gravy. They also have a weekend lineup of live bands running the gamut from cover to quirky and independent, including some of the best Texas pop and twang in the state. (*$, (979) 846–8806, fitzwillysbar.com*) ❷ **Halo Bar:** Halo is the closest thing you'll find here to a NYC-style dance club. Party-animals and dance-monsters of all stripes shake the junk in their trunk at this multilevel video bar and dance club. On the first floor are a bar, pool tables, and 11 flat-screen monitors featuring the latest dance mix videos. The second level offers engaging lighting and sound including multiple disco balls, a laser system, plus fire and smoke effects. (*$, (979) 823-6174, halobcs.com*) ❸ **Revolution Café & Bar:** It isn't all country music here in College Station. Revolution specializes in live jazz, funk, and reggae, with a crowd that's today's version of hipsters and beatniks. The interior is a giant step up from your normal roadhouse décor, with windows draped with wine-colored curtains and upholstered sofas and chairs that beg you to lounge on them. There's a full bar, a lengthy list of premium coffees and sandwiches, and a large patio. (*$, (979) 823-4044, revolutioncafeandbar.com*)

❹ **Texas Hall of Fame:** This is a cavernous country dance hall with a full bar and lots of hats and boots. Be prepared for a mass of bodies flooding the dance floor, scooting their boots to live bands or DJs. If you're looking for an authentic, rowdy Texas dance experience, this place is a good bet. (*$, (979) 822–2222, texashallof fame.net*)

Shopping

❶ **Aggieland Depot:** This is for the more refined Aggie shopper, with framed Aggie art, jewelry, custom framing, and higher-end versions of office and home décor. All have carefully placed TAMU logos. (*(979) 695-1422, aggieland-depot.com*) ❷ **Aggieland Outfitters:** With two locations, Aggieland has a cornucopia of TAMU stuff to add to your Aggie collection. There's plenty of merchandise for him, her, Junior, and even Fluffy. Their inventory ranges from flip-flops to auto supplies. (*(979) 764-4445, aggielandoutfitters.com*) ❸ **Antique Rose Emporium:** Okay, it's a little different from your normal store, but that's the fun. About 30 miles south of A&M, the Emporium is a large nursery dedicated to preserving old, antiquated varieties of rose—which are often easier to grow and more disease-resistant than modern roses. While you can buy some great roses here, the main draw is their beautiful, multi-acre themed gardens featuring hundreds of roses, perennials, herbs, and native plants. (*(800) 441-0002, antiquerose emporium.com*) ❹ **The Garden District:** This is a good place to enjoy wares from Bryan's local, independent merchants. The District has a walkable, garden-like atmosphere, with shops and cafés. **The Little Red Schoolhouse** will keep you clothed in the latest styles, while **Pygmalion** puts one-of-a-kind jewels on your fingers and toes. If you're hot and tired, **The T Garden Café** can refresh with a glass of wine or iced tea, as well as a sandwich or dessert.

TEXAS TECH

Texas Tech University: 27,000 students
Lubbock, TX: pop. 209,737
Jones AT&T Stadium: seats 53,000
Colors: Scarlet and Black
Nickname: Red Raiders
Mascot: The Masked Rider, Raider Red
Phone: (806) 742-3811

Visiting RVs can park in United Spirit Arena early as 5:30 Friday at no charge. All must depart by Sunday morning. Tailgating starts upon arrive and runs until departure. Keep all gear within parking space; don't block traffic.

Shuttle Info: Citibus provides shuttle from United Spirit Arena, $5 per person.

Red Raiders Media Partner: 1340-AM KKAM

In 1923 Texas legislators planned to open a branch of Texas A&M University in West Texas. But not everyone agreed that was the best route to go, and opposition grew. The issue wasn't if there should be a university in West Texas, but whether it should be associated with Texas A&M.

In the end, the answer was no, and the state created Texas Technological College.

Now the question was where to locate it. Several cities wanted the university, but Lubbock wanted it more. Its citizens lined the streets cheering as the selection committee drove by. This enthusiasm paired with more nuts-and-bolts factors led Lubbock to be selected on the first ballot. When the city learned it was selected, it threw a party that hosted 30,000 people. Lubbock had just a few thousand residents at the time.

The school opened in 1925 with 914 students. By the 1960s it was a much bigger school with a much broader focus. Administrators didn't feel Texas

Technological College fit anymore for a university teaching curriculum ranging from agriculture to engineering, arts and sciences to home economics. At most universities across the country, this type of name change wasn't a big deal. At Texas Technological College, it was.

Several names were suggested, including Texas State University (a front runner), the Texas University of Arts, Science and Technology, and University of the Southwest. But the school, and alumni, wanted to maintain the school's double-T logo, so the compromise winner was Texas Tech University. Many students and faculty hated it.

There were campus protests and rumors that many of the faculty would quit if the name were changed. One student wrote to the student paper, "Tech to me is a coined word and does not dignify this fine institution." There were several student votes in favor of Texas State University. One student, in reference to the school and legislators ignoring the opinions of students and faculty, suggested the school be called the University of Moscow at Lubbock.

But the school's Board of Directors wasn't swayed and took Texas Tech University to the legislature, which passed it and sent the name to the governor, who signed the bill in July 1969.

Texas Tech's football program began with a little controversy, too. On October 3, 1925, Tech played its first game against McMurry University, and while the details are a little sketchy, it ended in a scoreless tie that Tech fans didn't agree with.

During the next several decades the team was pretty lackluster, both in performance and fan spirit. There have been some runs where the Red Raiders put together winning seasons and appeared in bowl games (including 11-win seasons in 1953 and 1973), but most feel the program really took off in 2000 when Mike Leach came to Lubbock.

Coach Leach has led the Red Raiders on a run of winning seasons and bowl game appearances every year (as of the start of the 2007 season when this book went to print). As a result Red Raider fans turn out in much larger numbers to tailgate and watch the games. So many more that the school had to add more seats to Jones AT&T Stadium.

Texas Tech also left its footprint on the national college football system. Former Texas Tech University Athletic Council chairman Dr. J. William Davis was concerned about coaches signing recruits from other colleges, so he created the National Letter of Intent to keep that from happening. The form was adopted by the Colleges Commissioners Association in 1964.

School Mascot

How does the Texas Tech Doggies sound?

It would have happened if not for the football coach's wife, who felt Matadors was a better name, representing the Spanish influence on campus found in the architecture.

Tech was the Matadors in 1932 when a local sports writer, writing of the team's great season, referred to the team as "The Red Raiders from Texas Tech, terror of the Southwest this year…"

The name caught on, and by 1936 Matadors had been replaced by Red Raiders.

Texas Tech's first mascot wasn't a dog, a matador, or a Red Raider. It was a black calf. It was donated to the team after the school's inaugural football win—which was the third game of 1925. They branded the calf with the 30–0 winning score, and the rest of the season he attended games and at halftime fans of the opposing team would try to ride him without being bucked off. None was successful.

At the end of the season, they slaughtered the animal and barbecued it for the team. The idea was to tan the hide and put it in the team's trophy room. But the hair fell off, so that never happened.

In 1936 another mascot was unveiled, sort of. It actually started as a prank when the head yell leader "dreamed up this Red Raider thing," as fellow student George Tate later recalled. Tate borrowed a horse from the school barn, donned a scarlet satin cape and a mask, and led the football team onto the field. It was a prank, but he did it a few more times that season. His identity was a secret, and the horse and rider disappeared at the end of the season.

It wasn't until 1953 when Tech's football coach asked a student to resurrect the Masked Rider. At the time the team was headed to the Gator Bowl and hoping to be invited into the Southwest Conference. The other teams had mascots, and the coach thought it would help if Tech had one, too.

So at the 1954 Gator Bowl, the student (named Joe Kirk Fulton for you trivia buffs) rode Blackie onto the field, followed by the team. At first the crowd sat in stunned silence. Then it erupted into cheers. As a sports writer for the *Atlanta Journal* wrote, "No team in any bowl game ever made a more sensational entrance."

Tech was invited to, and joined, the Southwest Conference. History isn't clear on whether the mascot was the deciding factor.

History is clear that a Southwest Conference rule initiated in the early 1970s is the reason Tech has a second mascot, Raider Red.

Texas Tech Fight Song

"Fight Raiders, Fight"

Fight, Raiders, Fight!
Fight, Raiders, Fight!
Fight for the school we love so dearly.
You'll hit 'em high,
you'll hit 'em low.
You'll push the ball across the goal,
Tech, Fight! Fight!
We'll praise your name,
Boost you to fame.
Fight for the Scarlet and Black.
You will hit 'em, you will wreck 'em.
Hit 'em, wreck 'em, Texas Tech!
And the victory bells will ring out.

The new rule prohibited teams from taking live animals to away games unless the home team allowed it. Students and administrators felt their opponents would rarely, if ever, allow it, so they created a costumed mascot based on a character cartoonist Dirk West drew (he also served as Lubbock's mayor). The Wild West character roams the sidelines during games and fires his pistols into the air after each Red Raider score.

Game-Day Traditions
Guns Up!

Like the other schools in the old Southwest Conference, Texas Tech has a traditional hand symbol fans use throughout the game to show their support. They call it "Guns Up!" and it's made by making a pistol with the forefinger and thumb of your right hand and holding up at an angle.

Will Rogers Statue

In 1950 Amon G. Carter, who founded the *Fort Worth Star-Telegram* and was a friend of Will Rogers, donated to Texas Tech a statue of Rogers riding his horse Soapsuds. He said the West Texas setting was perfect for such a statue of the humorist and actor.

The statue was well received, but, legend has it, there was controversy about where to put it.

The plan was to face it due west so Rogers could be riding off into the sunset. The problem was that meant the horse's posterior would face toward downtown Lubbock (local businesses didn't like that), and it would face the university entrance (students and administrators didn't like that).

The solution was to rotate the statue 23-degrees to the northwest. Now Soapsuds's rear faces to the southeast toward Texas A&M University.

Before every home game the school's spirit club, the Saddle Tramps, wraps the statue with red crepe paper to support the Red Raiders.

Visiting Texas Tech

Lubbock has grown into a city of more than 200,000, but it still holds on to its small town hospitality and West Texas charm. The city is named for Thomas Lubbock, a Confederate officer, Texas Ranger, and signer of the Texas Declaration of Independence. In addition to being home to Texas Tech and Lubbock Christian University, it is one of the largest cotton-growing regions on the planet, producing up to 3 million bales of cotton a year. It is also the hometown of several people you've listened to on the radio, from Buddy Holly to Mac Davis to Natalie Maines (of Dixie Chicks fame).

Where to Stay

❶ **Arbor Inn & Suites:** This all-suite inn gives travelers large, well-lit one- and two-room suites with a variety of bed options (two queens, single king, bunk beds for kids) and well-appointed bathrooms with upscale toiletries. Other traveler treats include home-baked cookies and lemonade, and a complimentary breakfast on weekends with waffles, biscuits and gravy, fruit, and more. Rooms run $149–$179 during football weekends. (*(806) 722-2726, arborinnand suites.com*) ❷ **Broadway Manor:** Located in Lubbock's historic Overton District just a few blocks from Texas Tech, this attractive B&B has five uniquely theme-decorated guest rooms with private baths. Try the Siamese Garden room for some Oriental glamour, or the Wild West room for, well, you know. Depending on the room, rates are $99–$125 during football weekends, and require a two-night stay. (*(877) 504-8223, broadwaymanor.net*) ❸ **Camelot Village RV & Mobile Home Park:** Yes, there are permanent residents here, but they don't take up all of the 187 sites. All offer full utility hookups, the sites are clean, and visitors say this is the most pleasant park in the area. The park is well laid out, and sites are roomy and level. Sites are available for $20.50. (*(800) 354-9230,*

evergreenmh.com/CV/Default.htm) ❹ **The Dawkins House:** This American Foursquare/Craftsman-style home served as Texas Tech's College Club House during the 1930s. Today, it offers three well-furnished, comfortable guest rooms with a well-heeled, vintage look. Two guest rooms share a hall bath; the other has a private bath. Breakfasts are full meals ranging from Italian herb frittatas to Texas-style scrambled eggs 'n' ham with biscuits and gravy. Rooms are $75–$125, with a two-night minimum stay required on football weekends. (*(877) 765-9882, dawkinshousebnb.com*) ❺ **Koko Inn:** Koko has a relaxed style and an almost tropical vibe, with a large redwood deck surrounding a heated indoor pool and lots of plant life. Rooms are available as kings, doubles, or studios. Rooms are $90 for really big football games; and from $65 to $70 for other football weekends. (*(800) 782-3254, lubbockhospitality.com/koko*) ❻ **Woodrow House:** Within walking distance of campus, this large brick house was built specifically to be a B&B. There are seven rooms, each with a private bath. Rooms are named, and furnishings are themed around the name. For example, the Lone Star Room has Western-style furnishings, and the Alumni Room has Texas Tech bedspreads and a customized bed. A favorite room is actually a refurbished, red Santa Fe caboose, which functions like a miniapartment. Rooms are $95, and the caboose is $115 per night. Football weekends require a Friday and Saturday stay. (*(806) 793-3330, woodrowhouse.com*)

Where to Eat

TAILGATER SUPPLIES: ❶ Alternate Food Co-op: They have a large selection of natural foods, offering organic produce, bulk organic herbs and spices, organic package goods, dairy, and breads. As a cooperative store, the emphasis here is on good health through wholesome foods and service to the community. (*(800) 523-6601*) ❷ Lubbock Farmers' Market: They're a co-op of growers offering their own locally grown, fresh vegetables and fruit. The market is open until October on Tuesdays, Thursdays, and Saturdays from 7 a.m. until everything's sold out. It's also known as the Lubbock South Slide Farmers' Market. (*lubbockfarmersmarket.com*)

SPORTS BARS: ❸ Bleacher's Sports Café: Watch your favorite team on more than 30 TVs. This place is huge, so you'll find a seat even on the most crowded game days. The kitchen turns out a good ribeye steak, but the queso burger—a

big, messy, juicy burger covered with spicy queso cheese and all the fixin's—is a crowd favorite. (*$, (806) 744-7767, bleachersportscafe.com*) ❹ Jake's Sports Bar: With more than 60 TVs, Jake's is quickly becoming a Lubbock game-day favorite. There's plenty of sports to watch, and a menu with a low-carb section and some classic Tex-Mex in addition to the usual wings, burgers, and fried cheese apps. If your team's losing check out Jack's Back Room in the rear, with live music almost every Thursday, Friday, and Saturday night. (*$, (806) 687-5253, jakes-sportscafe.com*) ❺ Moose Magoo's: This is just a good ol' sports bar, full of fans drinking beer, playing pool, and watching the game. There are 14 TVs, including a wide-angle HDTV, 5 pool tables, and trivia games galore. Their Texas-sized menu's full of deep-fried appetizers, salads, and everything from burgers to mahi-mahi. Try the grilled tequila-lime shrimp off the "Sizzlin' Sensations" section. (*$, (806) 745-5005, moosemagoos.com*)

RESTAURANTS: ❻ Bryan's Steaks: Its strong suit is value for your dollar—try their 12-ounce New York strip steak for under $10. Bryan's corn fritters (you've never had corn fritters?) are crispy and creamy and worth driving across town for. You get all this while kicking back to enjoy Bryan's down-home cowboy-style atmosphere. Read this part carefully: bring cash; they don't take checks or credit cards. (*$, (806) 744-5491*) ❼ **La Diosa Cellars:** This is the place to stop for lunch (or dinner). This bistro coffee bar café may be the only winery in the country that operates within a city limits. Inside, La Diosa looks like a tropical vision of Mexico, with brilliantly colored walls, paintings, and chairs upholstered in every color from lipstick red to turquoise blue. Their menu is just as fun with wraps, paninis, and tapas. Try the Josephine wrap—a tomato-basil tortilla wrapped around roasted chicken, grilled peppers, onions, and jack cheese, served with black beans and pico de gallo. (*$, (806) 744-3600, ladiosacellars.com*) ❽ **Manna Bread & Wine:** This is a cozy, hip Southwestern-flavored bistro with a good wine selection, and a menu full of inventive Texas-chic food. Try entrées like tortilla-encrusted chicken in a smoked paprika cream sauce. Better yet, explore their tapas menu, with creations like beef-cheek empañadas. Inside, diners sit in one of two pleasant brick-walled dining rooms with tiled floors and a few funky touches (like a polka-dotted chicken) here and there. (*$–$$, (806) 791-5600, mannabreadandwine.com*)

❾ **Orlando's:** It's one of those places that make you feel like you're in someone's home. This is a Lubbock favorite for Italian food, with a fun blending of Southwestern and Italian flavors. Try the chicken linguine with olive oil, Parmesan cheese, toasted almonds, and a hint of green chile. Locals tell you to save room for their spumoni. (*$, (806) 797-8646, orlandos.com*)

Daytime Fun

❶ **The Buddy Holly Center:** If you're a rock 'n' roll fan, this terrific museum is a must-see. If you're not a big rocker, it's still worth visiting. Not surprisingly, the permanent exhibit about Buddy Holly's life and music is the centerpiece of this facility. But it's not the only pony in the show; it also houses an art gallery and the Texas Musicians Hall of Fame. Both the art gallery and the Hall of Fame are good enough to merit visits all on their own. (*$, (806) 775-3560, buddyhollycenter.org*) ❷ **Cap*Rock Winery:** Four miles south of Lubbock, at U.S. 87 South and Woodrow Road, this award-winning winery uses vinifera grapes to produce chardonnays, cabernet sauvignons, and other wines. It's one of the most attractive wineries you'll find anywhere with a Southwestern mission-style building whose elegant tasting room includes 14-foot ceilings, a stone fireplace, and a green marble-top bar. Free tours and samples are available throughout the week. (*Free, (806) 863-2704, caprockwinery.com*)

❸ **Mackenzie Park:** This is a pretty park that's jammed with fun things to do. There's Prairie Dog Town, a walled-in field serving as a sanctuary for prairie dogs. It's riddled with burrows and full of comic little ground squirrels that'll keep you entertained for quite a while, on an active day. If you have kids or if you're in touch with your own inner kid, visit Joyland Amusement Park and experience one of their stomach-dropping rides. There's a golf course, a sculpture garden, horse trails, and more. (*Free–$, (806) 775-2687, parks.ci.lubbock. tx.us/index.htm*)

Nighttime Fun

❶ **50th Street Caboose:** This family-friendly nightspot was the first restaurant in Lubbock to serve fajitas. It also has its own midway with more than 100 games and a redemption center stocked full of toys, novelties, and giant stuffed animals. That's the fun quotient. The full menu has a Mexican slant to it, with lots of Tex-Mex classic dishes. They also feature two separate Happy Hours, one daily from 4 to 7 p.m., the second from 9 to 11 p.m., Sunday through Thursday. (*$, (806) 796-2240, cabooseonline.com*) ❷ **The Blue Light:** Located in the historic Depot District on Buddy Holly Avenue. This live music venue has performances, usually with a Texas country or Texas rock flavor. Acts tend to be emerging local and regional musicians and performers. (*$, (806) 762-1185, thebluelightlive.com*) ❸ **Cactus Theater:** Originally built to be a second-run movie theater, this is the centerpiece of Lubbock's performing arts scene. It's not so much that it's fancy and impressive, as it is constantly busy with shows ranging from doo-wop bands like The Platters to musicals like *Smoke on the Mountain*. The theater is active Friday through Sunday, and also presents live, nonmusical theater, like *The Odd Couple* and other classics. (*$$–$$$, (806) 762-3233, cactustheater.com*) ❹ **Texas Café and Bar:** aka the Spoon, this place features everything from local cover bands to national recording artists. Texas Blues is the Spoon's specialty, but occasionally you'll find anything from country to heavy metal. The Spoon also holds a legendary Sunday night jam, which was originally started by C. B. "Stubbs" Stubblefield and Jesse "Guitar" Taylor. The tradition continues today with musicians from all over West Texas coming to share their talents in front of an open mic. (*$, (806) 792-8544, texascafeandbar.net*)

Shopping

❶ **Boot City:** It's Texas, and Boot City has what every cowboy or cowgirl needs—and lots of it. In fact, they've got one of the largest selections of boots and Western wear on the South Plains. You can also get hats, buckles, accessories, and Western-themed artwork. (*(806) 797-8782, bootcity.com*)

❷ **Hulla B'lu:** This is a shopper's paradise, full of unique treasures for house and home. You can find some good dishware (if you're in the market) as well as lots of odds and ends. The handmade ceramic and furniture pieces by Mackenzie Childs are worth a look. (*(806) 749-4258, hullablu.com*) ❸ **KK's Craft & Antique Mall:** This is the place where local people come to sell their wares, and customers come from all around for good merchandise at fair prices. It's more of a flea market than an antique mall, so be prepared to find anything from socks to wristwatches to silk flowers. Don't worry . . . they have antiques, too. (*(806) 795-6169, kkcraft.com*) ❹ **Texas Tech University Bookstore:** If there's a double-T or a Red Raider on it, it's here. You can even pick up a ceramic Texas Tech cookie jar designed like a French chef. You'll find them in the Student Union Building. (*(800) 377-7329, texastech.bkstore.com*)

RECIPES

Appetizers

Soups & Salads

Sides

Main Dishes

Sweet Treats

Appetizers

CHILI CON QUESO

INGREDIENTS:
1 large onion, chopped
1 large green pepper, chopped
2 tablespoons butter or margarine
2 pounds process cheese spread
1 (10 ounce) can tomatoes and diced green chiles

DIRECTIONS:
Sauté onion and pepper in butter or margarine until soft. Cut cheese into chunks for easier melting. Using low heat, add cheese and melt, stirring constantly. Add tomatoes and green chiles and blend thoroughly. Let mixture heat to blend flavors, but do not boil. Serve with corn chips.

Yields 30 or more servings

Recipe from Aggies, Moms and Apple Pie *cookbook, courtesy of Texas A&M University Press*

TEXAS CAVIAR

INGREDIENTS:
2 cans black beans, drained
2 cans black-eyed peas, drained
2 cans Shoe Peg corn, drained
2 cans tomatoes with green chiles
1 bunch cilantro, chopped
1 green bell pepper, chopped
1 yellow bell pepper, chopped
1 red bell pepper, chopped
1 purple onion, chopped
1 or 2 jalapeño chiles, finely chopped
¼ cup red wine vinegar
¼ cup lime and chili vinegar
Salt and black pepper to taste
Cayenne pepper to taste
Chili powder to taste

DIRECTIONS:
Combine the black beans, black-eyed peas, Shoe Peg corn, and tomatoes with green chiles, cilantro, green bell pepper, yellow bell pepper, red bell pepper, onion, jalapeño chiles, red wine vinegar, lime and chili vinegar, salt, black pepper, cayenne pepper, and chili powder in a bowl and mix well. Chill, covered, for 8 to 10 hours; drain. Serve with corn chips or tortilla chips.

Yields 30 servings

Recipe from A Perfect Setting *cookbook, courtesy of the Junior League of Lubbock*

REUBEN DIP

INGREDIENTS:
1 can sauerkraut, undrained
3 packages corned beef or ½ pound fresh corned beef, cooked, chopped
8 ounces Thousand Island dressing
1 pound Swiss cheese, shredded

DIRECTIONS:
Mix sauerkraut, corned beef, cheese, and Thousand Island dressing
together, and heat in crock pot. Serve with rye crackers.

Yields 20 servings

Barb Negri, Iowa State University

FRESH ASPARAGUS SPEARS WITH DIP

INGREDIENTS:
2 pounds fresh asparagus spears
Assorted fresh vegetables (optional)

DIP INGREDIENTS:
2 cups asparagus, cooked
½ cup sour cream
¼ teaspoon hot pepper sauce
¼ teaspoon dill
½ teaspoon salt

DIRECTIONS FOR ASPARAGUS DIP:
Cook the asparagus in a small amount of water until tender. Drain. Put the asparagus, sour cream, hot sauce, dill, and salt in a blender or food processor. Blend until smooth. Cover and chill for 1 hour.

DIRECTIONS:
Wash the asparagus to remove sand. Trim the bottoms to the tender part of the stalk and arrange the spears on a large platter. You may include other fresh vegetables such as cherry tomatoes, cucumber sticks, broccoli tops, snow peas, zucchini, and carrots. Serve with Asparagus Dip.

OPTION:
If you don't care for raw asparagus, blanch the asparagus in boiling water for 20 seconds. Remove and place in a pan of ice water to cool. Drain and chill. This will remove the "grassy" taste, but leave the spears firm for dipping.

Recipe from The Kansas Cookbook: Recipes from the Heartland, *by Frank Carey and Jayni Naas, published by the University Press of Kansas © 1989*

HOT CRACKER SPREAD

INGREDIENTS:
1 (8-ounce) package cream cheese, softened
2 tablespoons milk
½ cup sour cream
¼ cup chopped green peppers
2 tablespoons onion flakes
1 (2 ½-ounce) jar dried beef, snipped
½ teaspoon garlic salt
¼ teaspoon pepper

TOPPING:
¼ cup nuts, chopped
2 tablespoons butter
¼ teaspoon salt (optional)

DIRECTIONS:
Combine ingredients for the spread and spoon into dish for baking and serving. Mix the nuts, butter, and salt, and heat until crisp. Sprinkle on top of cheese mixture. Bake approximately 20 minutes at 350°F. Serve warm with crackers.

Yields about 2 cups

Recipe from Aggies, Moms and Apple Pie *cookbook, courtesy of Texas A&M University Press*

FRESH TOMATO SALSA

INGREDIENTS:
2 cups chopped tomatoes
½ cup finely diced red onion
2 serrano or jalapeño chiles, finely minced
½ cup chopped fresh cilantro
1 teasoon salt
⅛ teaspoon white pepper
2 tablespoons lime juice

DIRECTIONS:
Combine all ingredients and toss gently to mix. Cover and let stand for about an hour to blend flavors. Serve with chips for an appetizer, or as a topping on grilled steak, chicken, or burgers.

Yields about 3 cups

Sally Barclay, Iowa State University

BEAN DIP

INGREDIENTS:
1 can drained black beans
1 can drained pinto beans
1 can drained white corn
1 can drained yellow corn
4 green onions, chopped
½ bottle light Italian dressing
White granulated sugar to taste

DIRECTIONS:
Drain and rinse beans and corn. Mix all ingredients in a bowl; cover and let sit in the refrigerator at least an hour. If desired, add more sugar or Italian dressing. Serve with tortilla chips or as a topping to your favorite grilled meat.

Yields about 40 servings

Justine Hoover, Iowa State University, adapted from a recipe by Rollie Weber, Iowa State University

HOT CHILI BEEF DIP

INGREDIENTS:
2 pounds lean ground beef
1 onion, chopped
1 sweet green pepper, chopped
1 (8-ounce) jar taco sauce, as hot as you like it
1 (15-ounce) can tomato sauce
1 (11-ounce) can condensed cheddar cheese soup

DIRECTIONS:

Brown ground beef, onion, and green pepper in skillet; pour off drippings. Add remainder of ingredients and simmer 10 to 15 minutes. Pour into heatproof bowl and serve hot with tortilla chips.

Yields 50 servings

Lois Heckert, Iowa State University

GRILLED JALAPEÑO PEPPERS

INGREDIENTS:

10 jalapeño peppers
8-ounce package cream cheese
12-ounce package bacon

DIRECTIONS:

Cut peppers in half length wise. Take out the seeds and only put 3 to 5 seeds back in the halves. Fill each half with cream cheese. Wrap each half with a piece of uncooked bacon. Put nonstick aluminum foil on the grill (making sure to turn up the edges like a pan so the grease doesn't run off). Place the peppers on the grill. Cook until bacon is just about done. You can turn them upside down first for a few minutes and then turn them so the pepper is on the bottom for the rest of the cooking if you like your bacon a little more done.

Yields 10 servings

Teresa Schierer, Iowa State University

EASY CYCLONE CHICKEN ON A STICK

INGREDIENTS:
1 bottle maple syrup
1 bottle hot sauce
6 chicken breasts cut into 1 ½-inch chunks
Wooden skewers

DIRECTIONS:
Combine 1 ⅓ cup maple syrup with ⅔ cup hot sauce (a 2-to-1 ratio) and adjust to taste. Combine chunks of chicken and marinade. Using the 2-to-1 ratio, mix up more marinade, if necessary, to fully coat chicken. Cover and marinate in refrigerator over night. Put chicken on wooden skewers. Grill over medium coals until chicken is cooked through.

NOTE:
This is the ultimate tailgating food. No condiments required. Eat with one hand and hold your favorite beverage with the other.

Yields 6 to 8 servings

Tim and Lori Wignall, Iowa State University

RASPBERRY "AGGIE SALAD"

INGREDIENTS:
1 large package (6 ounces) raspberry gelatin (regular or sugar-free)
2 cups boiling water
1 (10-ounce) box frozen raspberries, partially thawed, with juice
1 (16-ounce) can applesauce
½ cup sour cream
1 tablespoon sugar

DIRECTIONS:
Add boiling water to gelatin, stirring until dissolved. Stir in raspberries; crush with spatula or potato masher. Add applesauce and mix well. Pour into 13x9-inch glass baking dish and chill. When firm, top with sour cream mixed with sugar.

Yields 8 to 10 servings

Recipe from Aggies, Moms and Apple Pie *cookbook, courtesy of Texas A&M University Press*

GREEN AND GOLD MARINATED SALAD

INGREDIENTS:
¾ cup vinegar
¼ cup extra-virgin olive oil
¼ cup corn oil
1 cup sugar
2 tablespoons water
Salt and pepper to taste
2 cans tiny green peas, drained
2 cans Shoe Peg corn, drained
1 small jar pimento, drained
5 green onions, chopped
6 ribs celery, chopped
1 green bell pepper, chopped

DIRECTIONS:
Combine the vinegar, olive oil, corn oil, sugar, water, salt, and pepper in a saucepan. Cook over medium heat until the sugar is dissolved, stirring frequently. Let stand until cool. Combine the peas, corn, pimento, green onions, celery, and bell pepper in a bowl and mix well. Pour the vinegar mixture over the vegetable mixture and mix well. Chill, covered, for 12 hours or longer.

Yields 20 servings

Recipe from A Perfect Setting *cookbook, courtesy of the Junior League of Lubbock*

BROCCOLI SALAD

INGREDIENTS:
2 (10 ounces each) packages frozen chopped broccoli
1 cup sliced green olives
½ cup chopped celery
3 hard-cooked eggs, chopped
Mayonnaise to moisten, ¼–½ cup

DIRECTIONS:
Defrost broccoli and drain thoroughly. Combine with olives, celery, and hard-cooked eggs. Add mayonnaise to taste. Refrigerate 3–4 hours before serving. (Ed. Note: Sliced water chestnuts make a good, crunchy addition to this salad.)

Yields 6 to 8 servings

Recipe from Aggies, Moms and Apple Pie *cookbook, courtesy of Texas A&M University Press*

HARVEST TOMATO SALAD

INGREDIENTS:
3 cups fresh tomatoes
2 medium cucumbers
1 mild onion
¼ cup cider vinegar
¼ cup sugar

DIRECTIONS:
Peel and chop tomatoes, cucumbers, and onion and place them in a large bowl. Combine cider vinegar and sugar in a small bowl. Stir to dissolve the sugar and pour over the vegetables. Stir gently, cover, and refrigerate until ready to serve. Add salt only when serving because salad will become too watery if added sooner.

Yields 6 to 8 servings

Recipe from The Kansas Cookbook: Recipes from the Heartland, *by Frank Carey and Jayni Naas, published by the University Press of Kansas © 1989*

GREEN CHILE CHOWDER

INGREDIENTS:
¼ to ½ cup jalapeño chiles, seeded and minced
¼ cup frozen green chiles, thawed and chopped
1 cup finely chopped onion
3 or 4 potatoes, cut into ½-inch pieces
2 garlic cloves, minced
4 cups chicken broth

½ teaspoon salt
⅓ cup margarine
⅓ cup all-purpose flour
3 cups milk
1 cup (4 ounces) shredded cheddar cheese

DIRECTIONS:

Combine the jalapeño chiles, green chiles, onion, potatoes, garlic, chicken broth, and salt in a stockpot over high heat. Bring to a boil. Reduce the heat and simmer for 20 minutes. Melt the margarine in a saucepan over low heat. Add the flour and cook for 3 minutes, whisking constantly. Drain the jalapeño chile mixture, reserving the jalapeño chile mixture and the liquid. Add the reserved liquid to the flour mixture. Cook over medium heat until thickened, whisking constantly. Add the milk and cook until thickened, stirring constantly. Remove from the heat. Add the reserved jalapeño chile mixture and mix well. Cook until heated through, stirring occasionally. Ladle into soup bowls. Sprinkle each serving with 2 tablespoons of the cheese.

Yields 8 servings

Recipe from A Perfect Setting *cookbook, courtesy of the Junior League of Lubbock*

Sides

YOGURT STUFFED POTATOES

INGREDIENTS:

4 large baking potatoes
¾ cup plain yogurt
½ teaspoon salt
¼ teaspoon pepper
⅓ to ⅔ cup milk, scalded
2 green onions, chopped
½ cup sharp cheddar cheese, shredded
3 tablespoons butter, melted

DIRECTIONS:

Wash potatoes and pierce them several times with a fork. Bake them at 400°F for about 1 to 1 ¼ hours, or until soft. Remove potatoes from the oven and cool for 10 minutes. Slice the potatoes open lengthwise and scoop out the insides, being careful not to tear the skins. Set the skins aside. Place potato in a mixing bowl and mash with a hand masher or electric mixer. Add the yogurt, salt, and pepper. Add the milk, as needed, until the potato mixture is smooth and light. Stir in the green onion and cheese. Spoon the potato mixture back into the shells. Top each potato half with about 1 teaspoon of melted butter. Place potato halves in a large baking dish. Bake uncovered at 400°F for 30 minutes or until tops are golden.

Yields 4 to 8 servings

Recipe from The Kansas Cookbook: Recipes from the Heartland, *by Frank Carey and Jayni Naas, published by the University Press of Kansas © 1989*

COACH'S FAVORITE JALAPEÑO CORN BREAD

INGREDIENTS:
1 cup buttermilk
1 cup yellow cornmeal
1 cup sifted all-purpose flour
3 tablespoons sugar
1 teaspoon salt
1 teaspoon baking powder
½ teaspoon baking soda
1 egg, beaten
¼ cup shortening, melted
1 (16-ounce) can corn, drained
2 cups (8 ounces) shredded cheddar cheese
3 jalapeño chiles, chopped

DIRECTIONS:
Combine the buttermilk, cornmeal, and flour in a bowl and mix well. Add the sugar, slat, baking powder, baking soda, egg, shortening, corn, cheese, and jalapeño chiles and mix well. Pour into greased 9x13-inch baking pan. Bake at 375°F for 30 minutes. You may substitute a different type of cheese for the cheddar.

Yields 15 servings

Recipe from A Perfect Setting *cookbook, courtesy of the Junior League of Lubbock*

GRILLED VEGETABLES

INGREDIENTS:
3 to 4 large potatoes
1 large onion
2 or more each of any other vegetables you like (bell peppers, carrots,
green beans, pea pods, etc.)
Favorite herbs (rosemary, thyme, garlic, etc.)

DIRECTIONS:
Wash and slice all vegetables. Grease 4 large sheets of tin foil with
cooking spray. Place half of the vegetables on 1 sheet of foil and half on
another. Sprinkle herbs on top of the vegetables, use as much or as little
as you would like. Place the other 2 sheets of tin foil on top of the
vegetables and tightly roll up each edge so the vegetables cannot fall out.
Grill until vegetable are tender, about 10–15 minutes on each side.

Yields 6 servings

*Justine Hoover, Iowa State University, adapted from a recipe by Dee Behr, Iowa
State University*

JULY FOURTH POTATO SALAD

INGREDIENTS:
3 pounds red potatoes, scrubbed
1 cup Italian salad dressing
4 eggs, hard-cooked
1 cup sliced celery

½ cup sliced green onions
1 cup mayonnaise
½ cup sour cream
1 ½ teaspoons horseradish mustard
1 teaspoon garlic salt
1 teaspoon celery seeds

DIRECTIONS:
Combine the potatoes and enough water to cover in a saucepan. Cook until tender; drain. Let stand until cool. Slice the potatoes. Combine the potatoes and salad dressing in a bowl and toss to coat. Chill, covered, for 8 to 10 hours. Drain the potatoes. Cut the eggs into halves and separate the egg whites and egg yolks; chop the egg whites. Combine the potatoes, celery, green onions, and egg whites in a bowl and mix well. Combine the mayonnaise, sour cream, horseradish mustard, garlic salt, and celery seeds in a bowl and mix well. Add to the potato mixture and mix gently. Spoon into a serving dish. Press the egg yolks through a sieve onto the top of the salad.

Yields 8 servings

Recipe from A Perfect Setting *cookbook, courtesy of the Junior League of Lubbock*

MARINATED MUSHROOMS

INGREDIENTS:
3 (4 ½-ounce) jars button mushrooms
½ cup tarragon vinegar
½ cup brown sugar
¼ teaspoon salt
½ tablespoon whole black pepper
1 bay leaf
1 clove garlic, sliced

DIRECTIONS:
Drain mushrooms, reserving liquid. Combine all ingredients except mushrooms, and bring to a boil in a small saucepan. Pour over mushrooms. Store in a tightly sealed glass jar in the refrigerator for 24 hours.

Yields 10 servings

Recipe from Aggies, Moms and Apple Pie *cookbook, courtesy of Texas A&M University Press*

ONIONS WITH HERBS AND BUTTER

INGREDIENTS:
4 medium yellow onions
¼ teaspoon marjoram
¼ teaspoon thyme
¼ teaspoon basil
¼ teaspoon tarragon
Salt and pepper to taste
½ cup butter

DIRECTIONS:
Skin the onions. From the top, make a crisscross cut ¾ of the way through each one. Place each onion on a large square of aluminum foil. Combine the marjoram, thyme, basil, and tarragon in a small bowl. Sprinkle ¼ teaspoon of the herb mixture over each onion. Sprinkle with salt and pepper to taste. Top each one with 2 tablespoons butter. Wrap the foil securely around each onion to seal in the juices. Place the onions over medium-hot coals on a covered grill and bake for 45 to 60 minutes, or until easily pierced with a knife and the juices begin to caramelize.

Yields 4 servings

Recipe from The Kansas Cookbook: Recipes from the Heartland, *by Frank Carey and Jayni Naas, published by the University Press of Kansas © 1989*

TEQUILA CORN

INGREDIENTS:
¼ cup minced shallots
1 small red bell pepper, finely chopped
1 tablespoon minced garlic
1 tablespoon olive oil
2 cans niblet corn
2 tablespoons tequila
1 tablespoon fresh lime juice
Salt to taste
2 cups heavy cream
¼ cup finely chopped fresh cilantro
12 cherry tomatoes, cut into quarters

DIRECTIONS:
Sauté the shallots, bell pepper, and garlic in the olive oil in a skillet over medium heat until tender. Add the corn, tequila, lime juice, and salt and mix well. Cook over medium-high heat for about 4 minutes, stirring frequently. Add the cream, cilantro, and cherry tomatoes and cook just until heated through, stirring occasionally.

Yields 6 servings

Recipe from A Perfect Setting *cookbook, courtesy of the Junior League of Lubbock*

BARBECUED SWEET CORN

INGREDIENTS:
6 ears of fresh sweet corn in the husks
Ice water
Salt (optional)

DIRECTIONS:
Pull back the husks, remove the silk, and replace the husk. Tie the husks with string or fine wire at the center and at the tip of the cob, making sure the kernels are covered. Place the ears of corn in a pan of ice water, salted if desired, and soak for 15 to 30 minutes. Drain the ears and place them directly over hot coals for 10 to 20 minutes, turning frequently, until the kernels are tender. Just before serving, remove the husks. If tied with wire, snip the hot wire with wire cutters, wearing gloves or using hot pads.

Yields 6 servings

Recipe from The Kansas Cookbook: Recipes from the Heartland, *by Frank Carey and Jayni Naas, published by the University Press of Kansas © 1989*

Main Dishes

SALMON BURGERS

INGREDIENTS:
1 (15 ½ ounce) can salmon, drained, skin removed, flaked
½ cup uncooked oatmeal
2 tablespoons reduced-calorie mayonnaise
½ cup chopped onion
2 to 3 egg whites
2 tablespoons lemon juice
1 tablespoon bottled horseradish or Dijon style mustard
4 hamburger buns

DIRECTIONS:
Mix all ingredients and shape into burgers (the mixture may be somewhat crumbly). Coat grill or skillet with cooking spray and add burgers. Cook until the burgers form a nice brown crust. Carefully flip and cook until that side also forms a crust. Serve on bun, if desired, with lettuce, tomato, and other condiments. Note: These are a healthful alternative to burgers and brats.

Yields 4 large burgers

Sally Barclay, Iowa State University

MESQUITE-SMOKED TURKEY

INGREDIENTS:
1 (8- to 10-pound) turkey
3 tablespoons butter or margarine
2 tablespoons meat rub (preferably Cavender's)

DIRECTIONS:
Arrange mesquite wood chips in a smoker. Preheat the smoker to 300°F and heat for 30 minutes. Remove and discard the packet from the turkey cavity. Rinse the turkey. Coat with the butter and rub with the meat rub. Smoke over indirect heat for 2 to 2 ½ hours. Wrap in heavy-duty foil. Bake at 250°F in the oven for 2 hours. You may grill the turkey on a gas grill instead. For a smoky flavor, soak the mesquite wood chips in water and wrap them in foil. Poke holes in the foil and place on the coals while grilling the turkey.

Yields 12 servings

Recipe from A Perfect Setting *cookbook, courtesy of the Junior League of Lubbock*

AUNT WANDA'S "GOOD" CHILI

INGREDIENTS:
4 pounds ground chili meat
2 large onions, chopped
4 cloves garlic, minced
1 large can (46 ounces) tomato juice
½ teaspoon crushed red pepper
5 teaspoons cumin
8 tablespoons chili powder
3 teaspoons salt
2 tablespoons masa harina, mixed with water

DIRECTIONS:
Cook meat, onion, and garlic until brown. Add tomato juice and bring to a boil. Reduce heat to simmer. Add red pepper, cumin, chili powder, and salt. Cook slowly for several hours. You may add water if needed during cooking. Mix masa harina with small amount of water; add for the last 30 minutes.

Yields 10 to 12

Recipe from Aggies, Moms and Apple Pie *cookbook, courtesy of Texas A&M University Press*

GRILLED TURKEY TENDERS

INGREDIENTS:
2 pounds turkey tenders
½ cup soy sauce
½ cup vegetable oil
6 ounces pineapple juice

DIRECTIONS:
Cut turkey tenders into 2- to 3-ounce pieces. Place turkey tenders in a
9x13-inch pan. Combine soy sauce, vegetable oil, and pineapple juice in a
medium mixing bowl. Pour marinade over turkey tenders. Marinate in
refrigerator from 1 hour up to over night. Grill turkey tenders until cooked
through.

Yields 10 to 12 servings

Jan Hoover, Iowa State University

CATTLEMEN'S PRIME RIB SPECIAL

INGREDIENTS:
1 (8-pound) boneless rib roast
Garlic-flavored olive oil*
Black pepper, coarsely ground

*To make garlic-flavored olive oil, place 2 whole peeled garlic cloves in ¼ cup high-quality olive oil. Cover and let sit for at least 24 hours.

DIRECTIONS:
Baste the rib roast with garlic-flavored olive oil and coat generously with black pepper. Brown on all sides (about 3 minutes per side) directly over hot coals. Continue cooking the meat over indirect heat. For this method, divide the hot coals, banking them on each side of a drip pan. Place the meat on the grill directly over the drip pan for indirect cooking. Cover the grill. Cooking time should be about 2 hours to 2 hours 40 minutes, or internal temperature is 155°F for medium rare meat. Add more hot coals as necessary after the first hour of cooking for even heat. Hickory chips may be added to the hot coals for hickory flavor.

Yields 8 to 10 servings

Recipe from The Kansas Cookbook: Recipes from the Heartland, *by Frank Carey and Jayni Naas, published by the University Press of Kansas © 1989*

TAILGATE OVEN SANDWICHES

INGREDIENTS:
Dijon mustard (optional)
Mayonnaise (optional)
2 (8-count) packages onion buns
1 pound deli ham, thinly sliced
1 pound deli turkey, thinly sliced
1 pound Swiss cheese, sliced

DIRECTIONS:
Spread Dijon mustard and mayonnaise over the cut sides of the buns.
Place 2 or 3 slices of ham or turkey and 1 slice of cheese on a bun half
and top with the remaining bun half. Wrap the sandwich in foil. Repeat
the procedure with the remaining buns, ham, turkey, and cheese. Bake at
300°F for 20 minutes. Transport the sandwiches in a cooler lined with
newspapers.

Yields 16 servings

Recipe from A Perfect Setting *cookbook, courtesy of the Junior League of Lubbock*

CHILI VERDE

INGREDIENTS:
1–1 ½ pounds round steak, cubed
Vegetable oil for sautéing
1 chopped onion
2 (4-ounce) cans diced green chiles
2 cloves garlic, chopped or mashed
Cumin to taste
2 cups water
2 bouillon cubes
1 package flour tortillas
1 (16-ounce) can refried beans
Monterey Jack cheese, shredded
Picante sauce to taste
Cheddar cheese, shredded

DIRECTIONS:
Cube round steak and sauté in small amount of oil. Add onions; stir until wilted. Add green chiles, garlic, and cumin. Add water and bouillon cubes, mixing well. Bring to a boil, lower heat, and simmer approximately 2 ½ hours. Add more water if necessary. Before serving, heat refried beans and shredded Monterey Jack cheese together. Steam flour tortillas (one way is to wrap them in foil and use a vegetable steamer over boiling water). Spread bean and cheese mixture over hot tortilla; add meat mixture down center of tortilla; add picante sauce and cheddar cheese. Fold ends in and roll.

Yields 4 to 6 servings

Recipe from Aggies, Moms and Apple Pie *cookbook, courtesy of Texas A&M University Press*

BOURBON-SPICED PORK TENDERLOINS

INGREDIENTS:
2 (1-pound) pork tenderloins
¼ cup bourbon
¼ cup soy sauce
¼ cup Dijon mustard
¼ cup packed brown sugar
¼ cup olive oil
1 ½ teaspoons ground ginger
2 teaspoons Worcestershire sauce
4 garlic cloves, minced

DIRECTIONS:
Place the pork in a nonreactive dish. Combine the bourbon, soy sauce, Dijon mustard, brown sugar, olive oil, ginger, Worcestershire sauce, and garlic in a blender or food processor and process until blended. Pour over the pork, turning to coat. Marinate, covered, in the refrigerator for 8 to 10 hours. Drain, reserving the marinade. Grill over high heat until seared on all sides; do not pierce the pork. Reduce the heat to medium. Grill for 25 minutes or until the pork is cooked through, basting frequently with the reserved marinade. Remove to a plate and cover with foil. Let stand for 10 minutes before slicing.

Yields 8 servings

Recipe from A Perfect Setting *cookbook, courtesy of the Junior League of Lubbock*

BARBECUED CHUCK ROAST

INGREDIENTS:

¼ cup olive oil

¼ cup red wine vinegar

¼ cup dry sherry

2 teaspoons soy sauce

1 teaspoon rosemary

½ teaspoon dry mustard

4 garlic cloves, minced

2 tablespoons catsup

1 ½ teaspoons steak sauce

½ teaspoon Worcestershire sauce

3 ½ to 4 pounds chuck roast, 2 ½ to 3 inches thick

DIRECTIONS:

Place the chuck roast in a wide bowl. Combine all other ingredients, except catsup, steak sauce, and Worcestershire sauce, and pour over the roast. Cover and refrigerate for a full 24 hours, turning the meat several times.

Remove the meat and drain, reserving the marinade. Add the ketchup, steak sauce, and Worcestershire sauce to the marinade. Stir well and baste the meat with the marinade before grilling.

Grill over hot coals, turning frequently and basting with the marinade every 5 to 10 minutes. Grill for about 30 to 40 minutes, or until desired doneness is achieved. (Internal temperature of 155°F for medium rare.)

Yields 6 servings

Recipe from The Kansas Cookbook: Recipes from the Heartland, *by Frank Carey and Jayni Naas, published by the University Press of Kansas © 1989*

AGGIE STEW

INGREDIENTS:
1 ½ to 2 pounds ground chuck
2 tablespoons margarine
1 large onion, diced
4 green onions, diced
3 stalks of celery, diced
1 small green pepper, diced
2 tablespoons chili powder
1 tablespoon sugar
1 (16-ounce) can tomatoes, with juice
1 (15-ounce) can chili-flavored red beans
1 (17-ounce) can whole kernel corn
6 medium potatoes, diced
Approximately 4 cups of water

DIRECTIONS:
Brown ground beef in margarine. Add other ingredients in order listed above. Bring to a boil. At this point, stew may be put into a slow cooker and left to simmer on low all day. Simmer until potatoes are done.

Yields 8 to 10 servings

Recipe from Aggies, Moms and Apple Pie *cookbook, courtesy of Texas A&M University Press*

SUMMER SPARERIBS

INGREDIENTS:
5 pounds boneless country-style pork spareribs
¼ cup Worcestershire sauce
1 ½ onions, chopped
1 cup packed brown sugar
1 cup ketchup
¼ cup vinegar
2 teaspoons dry mustard
1 ½ cups water
¼ teaspoon salt
1 teaspoon pepper

DIRECTIONS:
Arrange the spareribs in a 9x13-inch baking dish. Combine the Worcestershire sauce, onions, brown sugar, ketchup, vinegar, dry mustard, water, salt, and pepper in a bowl and mix well. Pour over the spareribs. Bake, covered, at 350°F for 2 ½ hours or until cooked through.

Yields 12 servings

Recipe from A Perfect Setting
cookbook, courtesy of the Junior
League of Lubbock

SAUSAGE AND CHEESE BAKE

INGREDIENTS:
1 tube (8) crescent rolls
1 pound sausage
1 (8-ounce) package mozzarella cheese, grated
2 tablespoons chopped green pepper
¼ cup chopped onion
4 eggs, slightly beaten
¼ cup milk
½ teaspoon salt
¼ teaspoon pepper
¼ teaspoon Italian seasoning

DIRECTIONS:
Open canned rolls and carefully unroll. Place in bottom of 9x13-inch casserole dish or pan. Press perforations and edges together, pushing to cover bottom of dish. Brown sausage and drain well. Put crumbled sausage on top of dough; add grated cheese, green pepper, and onions evenly over sausage. Beat eggs slightly; add milk, salt, pepper, and Italian seasoning. Pour over layered ingredients and bake 20–25 minutes in 375°F oven. Cool slightly before cutting.

Yields 24 bite-sized servings

Recipe from Aggies, Moms and Apple Pie *cookbook, courtesy of Texas A&M University Press*

BEEF TENDERLOIN FILLETS WITH SWEET RED PEPPER STUFFING

SWEET RED PEPPER STUFFING INGREDIENTS:
3 tablespoons butter
1 cup sweet red pepper, seeded and chopped
¼ cup onion, chopped
2 garlic cloves, minced
3 tablespoons Romano cheese, grated

TENDERLOIN INGREDIENTS:
4 beef tenderloin fillets about 1 ½ inches thick
2 teaspoons pepper, coarsely ground
1 cup cherry wood chips (optional)
Salt to taste

DIRECTIONS FOR STUFFING:
Melt the butter over low heat in a large frying pan. Add the chopped red pepper and onion. Cook slowly, stirring frequently, until the vegetables are tender, about 10 to 15 minutes. Add the garlic during the last few minutes of cooking. Remove the mixture from the heat and cool slightly. Stir in the Romano cheese and set aside.

DIRECTIONS:
Make a deep horizontal slice in the side of each tenderloin fillet to form a pocket for stuffing. Do not cut completely through the meat. Fill each pocket with the stuffing mixture, about 2 to 4 tablespoons each. Close the openings with toothpicks to hold the stuffing inside. Put about ½ teaspoon of the pepper into both sides of each fillet. Place the cherry wood chips on a piece of aluminum foil. Seal tightly to make a foil packet. Poke a few holes in the foil to allow the smoke to escape. Place foil packet directly on

very hot coals. Replace the grid, arrange the tenderloin fillets over the hot coals, and cover grill. Cook for 5 minutes. Turn the fillets and salt top sides. Continue cooking for 3 to 5 minutes more, or until desired doneness is achieved. Remove toothpicks before serving.

Yields 4 servings

Recipe from The Kansas Cookbook: Recipes from the Heartland, *by Frank Carey and Jayni Naas, published by the University Press of Kansas © 1989*

RAIDER BARBECUE BRISKET

INGREDIENTS:

2 tablespoons liquid smoke
4 pounds lean beef brisket
1 tablespoon onion salt
1 tablespoon garlic salt
3 tablespoons brown sugar
1 cup ketchup
¼ cup water
½ teaspoon celery salt
1 tablespoon liquid smoke
2 tablespoons Worcestershire sauce
3 tablespoons prepared mustard
2 tablespoons red wine vinegar
Salt and pepper to taste

DIRECTIONS:

Pour 2 tablespoons liquid smoke evenly over the beef. Rub with the onion salt and garlic salt. Wrap in foil and chill for 8 to 10 hours. Place the beef in a roasting pan. Bake, covered, at 300°F for 5 to 6 hours or until cooked through. Let stand until cool. Slice the beef and return to the roasting pan.

Combine the brown sugar, ketchup, water, celery salt, 1 tablespoon liquid smoke, Worcestershire sauce, prepared mustard, vinegar, salt, and pepper in a saucepan. Bring to a boil, stirring constantly. Pour over the beef. Bake, covered for 1 hour or until heated through.

Yields 8 to 10 servings

Recipe from A Perfect Setting *cookbook, courtesy of the Junior League of Lubbock*

Sweet Treats

WHITE CHOCOLATE TRAIL MIX

INGREDIENTS:
10 ounces miniature pretzels
5 cups Crispix cereal
5 cups Multigrain Cheerios cereal
5 cups Golden Grahams cereal
1 cup mixed nuts
16 ounces crispy M&M's Chocolate Candies
12 ounces vanilla chips
3 tablespoons canola oil

DIRECTIONS:
Combine the pretzels, Crispix, Cheerios, Golden Grahams, nuts, and
M&M's in a bowl and mix well. Combine the vanilla chips and canola oil
in a microwave-safe bowl. Microwave on low until the vanilla chips are
melted, stirring frequently; do not burn. Pour over the pretzel mixture and
toss to coat. Spread on waxed paper and let stand until cool. Store in an
airtight container.

Yields 80 servings

Recipe from A Perfect Setting *cookbook, courtesy of the Junior League of
Lubbock*

PAWPAW BREAD

INGREDIENTS:
⅓ cup shortening
¾ cup sugar
2 eggs
1 ¾ cups all-purpose flour
1 teaspoon baking soda
½ teaspoon salt
¼ teaspoon cinnamon
¼ teaspoon ginger
¼ teaspoon nutmeg
1 cup pawpaws (3 to 4 pawpaws, available at local farmers' markets)

DIRECTIONS:
In a mixing bowl, beat the shortening and sugar together. Add the eggs and beat well.

Sift the dry ingredients together in a large bowl and set aside. Peel and seed the pawpaws and cut them into chunks. Place the chunks in a small bowl and mash with a fork. Beat the dry ingredients into the mixture alternately with the mashed pawpaws.

Pour the batter into a greased 9x5x3-inch loaf pan. Bake at 350°F for 45 to 50 minutes, or until an inserted toothpick comes out clean.

Yields 1 loaf

Recipe from The Kansas Cookbook: Recipes from the Heartland, *by Frank Carey and Jayni Naas, published by the University Press of Kansas © 1989*

PUPPY CHOW

INGREDIENTS:
2 cups (12 ounces) chocolate chips
1 cup peanut butter
½ cup (1 stick) margarine
1 package rice Chex cereal
1 (1-pound) package confectioners' sugar

DIRECTIONS:
Combine the chocolate chips, peanut butter, and margarine in a saucepan. Cook until melted, stirring constantly. Remove from the heat. Place the cereal in a large bowl or pan. Add the chocolate chip mixture and stir to coat. Add the confectioners' sugar and shake to coat. Store in an airtight container.

Yields 16 to 20 servings

Recipe from A Perfect Setting *cookbook, courtesy of the Junior League of Lubbock*

APPLE CRUMB PIE

INGREDIENTS:
3 cups sliced peeled Granny Smith apples
⅔ cup sugar
1 teaspoon ground cinnamon
1 (9-inch) unbaked pie shell
½ cup all-purpose flour
½ cup rolled oats
¼ cup chopped nuts
½ cup (1 stick) butter, softened

DIRECTIONS:
Combine apples, sugar, and cinnamon in a bowl and mix well. Pour into the pie shell. Combine flour, oats, nuts, and butter in a bowl and mix until crumbly. Sprinkle evenly over the filling. Bake at 350°F for 40 to 45 minutes or until brown.

Yields 8 servings

Recipe from A Perfect Setting *cookbook, courtesy of the Junior League of Lubbock*

THE ULTIMATE TAILGATER'S BIG 12 HANDBOOK

PECAN PIE

INGREDIENTS:
3 eggs, lightly beaten
½ cup granulated sugar
1 tablespoon brown sugar
½ teaspoon salt
2 tablespoons butter, melted
1 teaspoon vanilla extract
¾ cup dark corn syrup
2 cups pecans
1 (1-crust) pie pastry

DIRECTIONS:
Combine eggs, granulated sugar, brown sugar, salt, butter, vanilla, and corn syrup in a bowl and mix well. Stir in pecans. Fit the pie pastry into a 9-inch pie plate. Pour the pecan mixture into the pie shell. Bake at 325°F for 50 to 60 minutes.

Yields 6 to 8 servings

Recipe from A Perfect Setting *cookbook, courtesy of the Junior League of Lubbock*

RESOURCES

Before you head to the car, you may need to find the best place to get more information on throwing a great tailgate party, or where to find the stuff with which to do it. Of course, you'll find tailgating tips (including game-day and travel checklists), podcasts, videos, and recipes at both **theultimatetailgater.com** and **theultimatetailgatechef.com**, but there are also a number of other sources to help grow your tailgating knowledge.

You can find all sorts of helpful tools and information about tailgating from the **American Tailgaters Association** at atatailgate.com. The ATA is a national organization that promotes tailgating, offers members discounts on tailgating supplies and gear, reviews tailgating products, and more. I'm thrilled they endorse The Ultimate Tailgater books. Membership is free, and you can sign up online.

If you're looking for help getting tickets or finding a place to stay in any Big 12 city, **FanHub** can hook you up. They work with ticket brokers and hotel room wholesalers to find the best deals for traveling fans. They also have fan forums so you can learn more about the stadium and things to do in town, as well as pipe in with your own experiences and thoughts. You'll find it all at fanhub.com.

Of course, you'll also need tailgating gear if you want to do things like sit and eat. Don't worry, I'm here for you. From grills to frilly hats (be careful who you let see you wearing the frilly hat), there are thousands of resources online if you can't find anything in stores near you.

Grills & Accessories

Before buying it's a good idea to compare features and options to make sure you get the best grill for your style of tailgating. Some good sources of information and research are:

bbq.about.com/od/grills/index.htm?terms=grills
consumersearch.com/www/sports_and_leisure/gas-grill-reviews/index.html

With your newfound grill knowledge, you're ready to get your grill. Here are some sites for tailgating grills and accessories:

bbqgalore.com
brinkmann.net
campchef.com
campingworld.com
ducane.com
freedomgrill.com
grillingaccessories.com
grilllovers.com
homedepot.com
lowes.com
webergrills.com

Tents

All across the Big 12 you'll find a sea of tents outside the stadium. For many tailgaters a canopy is enough. But for others, tents with sides and other options make for the ultimate tailgate party. You can find a variety of tents on these Web sites:

canopycenter.com
elitedeals.com/nctatelocate.html
eurekatents.com
ezupdirect.com
kdkanopy.com
shopping.com/xGS-Tailgating_Tents

General Tailgating Supplies

From licensed products to coolers to tables to chairs to . . . you get the idea.

americantailgater.com

collegegear.com

footballfanatics.com

tailgatehq.com

tailgatepartyshop.com

tailgatetown.com

tailgatingsupplies.com

Party Decorations

To turn your parking spot into a parking lot party you need to dress it up. In addition to food, drinks, and friends, party lights, banners, and pompoms help.

4funparties.com

bulkpartysupplies.com

party411.com

partyoptions.net/party_supply/football-main-page.htm

partypro.com

partyshelf.com/football.htm

Big 12 Schools and Teams

If you'd like to learn more about any of the Big 12 schools and their athletic programs, you can visit these official sites. Many of the athletic sites also have links to additional statistics and news.

SCHOOL SITES

Baylor: baylor.edu

Colorado: colorado.edu

Iowa State: iastate.edu

Kansas: ku.edu

Kansas State: k-state.edu

Missouri: missouri.edu

Nebraska:	unl.edu
Oklahoma:	ou.edu
Oklahoma State:	okstate.edu
Texas:	utexas.edu
Texas A&M:	tamu.edu
Texas Tech:	ttu.edu

ATHLETIC SITES

Baylor:	baylorbears.cstv.com
Colorado:	cubuffs.com
Iowa State:	cyclones.com
Kansas:	kuathletics.cstv.com
Kansas State:	k-statesports.com
Missouri:	mutigers.cstv.com
Nebraska:	huskers.com
Oklahoma:	soonersports.com
Oklahoma State:	okstate.com
Texas:	texassports.com
Texas A&M:	aggieathletics.com
Texas Tech:	texastech.cstv.com

ALUMNI ASSOCIATION SITES

Baylor:	bayloralumni.com
Colorado:	cualum.org
Iowa State:	isualum.org
Kansas:	kualumni.org
Kansas State:	k-state.com
Missouri:	mizzou.com
Nebraska:	huskeralum.com
Oklahoma:	alumni.ou.edu
Oklahoma State:	okstatealumni.org
Texas:	texasexes.org
Texas A&M:	aggienetwork.com
Texas Tech:	texastechalumni.org

THE ULTIMATE TAILGATER'S BIG 12 HANDBOOK

Also by Stephen Linn

FOX Sports Tailgating Handbook
The Ultimate Tailgater's ACC Handbook
The Ultimate Tailgater's SEC Handbook
The Ultimate Tailgater's Big Ten Handbook
The Ultimate Tailgater's Pac-10 Handbook
The Ultimate Tailgater's Handbook
The Ultimate Tailgater's Travel Guide
The Ultimate Tailgater's Racing Guide

Available in stores and at **theultimatetailgater.com.**

Also on **theultimatetailgater.com** you'll find tailgating videos, podcasts, contests, and more!